Financing World Trade

The Crowell Economics Series

Raymond F. Mikesell

UNIVERSITY OF OREGON

Financing World Trade

An Appraisal of the
International Monetary System
and of Proposals for Reform

THOMAS Y. CROWELL COMPANY

NEW YORK · Established 1834

This book is part of the Crowell/Challenge Series,
prepared in cooperation with Challenge Communications, Inc.,
New York, N.Y., Haig Babian, Editor.

L. C. Card 79–77342

Series design by Klaus Gemming
Manufactured in the United States of America

THIS BOOK IS FOR IRENE

Preface

WRITING ON the international monetary system in 1967–1969 approaches financial journalism; important events relating to this subject have been occurring almost daily. Moreover, the immediate future promises no retardation of significant developments. However, I have endeavored to provide a framework for interpreting past and future changes in the institutions and policies that facilitate and influence international economic transactions.

In writing this book, I am especially indebted to Professor Henry N. Goldstein of the University of Oregon who nearly tore my first draft to pieces with his rigorous criticism (and might have done the same with this version had I permitted him to review it). I am also grateful to Dr. Howard S. Piquet, formerly of the Library of Congress, to Dr. Marshall D. Wattles of the University of Oregon, and to Drs. Philip P. Schaffner and John W. Tanner of the U.S. Treasury Department for their helpful comments; they are, however, in no way responsible for my errors of judgment or of fact. Finally, nothing of mine would be publishable save for the editorial labor of my wife, Irene.

Eugene, Oregon   R.F.M.
January 1969

Contents

Tables and Figures

Tables

Figures

1

The International Payments Mechanism

The Institutional Base

THE MODERN international payments mechanism must be viewed fundamentally in terms of institutional arrangements which have developed over several centuries. The pound sterling, during the nineteenth and twentieth centuries, and the dollar, after World War I, did not become universally accepted means of making international payments and achieve the status of international reserve assets merely because of their convertibility into gold, or because Britain and the United States adhered to certain principles of monetary management. They achieved preeminence because of the institutions which were created within these countries and because of the economic relationships of these countries with other countries. These institutions and institutional relationships include the banking systems, specialized financial intermediaries, the foreign exchange markets, a variety of short- and long-term capital markets, the trading relationships of Britain and the United States with the rest of the world, and the structure and pattern of their foreign investments.

The institutional basis for an international currency role is also related to the broad economic and political power of the country in question in world affairs. The currency of a minor power is an unlikely candidate for a key currency role. Thus, despite the prestige of the Swiss franc in terms of stability and soundness, based on a high ratio of gold reserves to the volume of domestic money and the political and economic stability of the country, the Swiss franc has not become an important international vehicle currency.[1] The growth of the British Empire during the eighteenth and nineteenth centuries laid the foundations for the pound sterling as an international currency, while the rapid emergence of the United States as a major world power and the leading creditor nation during and after World War I thrust the dollar into the predominant key currency position.

The Emergence of Sterling as a World Currency

The essential elements in modern international payments are the financing of trade in goods and services and the transfer of capital assets between countries without the use of specie or direct barter. The basic instruments for the modern international payments system were developed on the European continent long before sterling became an international currency. The bill of exchange was introduced in Italy in the twelfth century, and the Bank of Amsterdam and the Amsterdam Bourse financed commercial transactions between countries in the sixteenth and seventeenth centuries before the Bank of England was founded in 1694.[2] The development of a market for internal bills of exchange in England during the eighteenth century, and the support of this market by the Bank of England when funds were scarce, laid the foundation for the London discount market which in the nineteenth century discounted bills of exchange arising out of trade among nations throughout the world.[3] Thus, exporters in foreign countries shipping to third countries began drawing bills not on the foreign importer but on a British merchant banking house, and these bills were drawn in sterling.

The predominance of sterling as an international payments me-

[1] The terms "key currency" and "vehicle currency" are applied to currencies used widely as a means of payment and for invoicing in international trade. "Wide use" implies use in financing of trade between countries other than the country whose currency is involved. The term "reserve currency" is used for currencies employed as international monetary reserves.

[2] See J. B. Condliffe, *The Commerce of Nations* (New York: W. W. Norton, 1950), p. 148.

[3] A bill of exchange is a draft drawn by an exporter on an importer or on a bank or financial institution to which the exporter looks for payment.

dium was enhanced by the expansion of Britain's trade and investment in its dependencies. Close financial ties between Britain and the economically less developed areas under British control—which included a large portion of the non-European world in the early part of the nineteenth century—assured that sterling would become the international payments medium of these countries and that their local currency reserves would take the form of sterling assets. Indeed, branches of London banks served as the principal banking institutions of the British dependencies, and London became both a source of loans and a depository of funds for a large part of the world outside Europe. The growth of British investments both on the European continent and in the non-British developing regions of the nineteenth century also furthered the international role of sterling.[4]

It is worth noting that the foundations for the world currency role of sterling evolved during the long period of suspension of specie payments (1797–1821) occasioned by the Napoleonic Wars, and that sterling continued to function as an international currency even during later periods of inconvertibility of sterling into gold or dollars at a fixed rate through much of the twentieth century, including the periods 1914–1925 and 1931–1959.[5] Moreover, the relationship between sterling and gold has been changed several times during the twentieth century, and sterling fluctuated freely without a gold parity between 1931 and 1939.

The Role of the U.S. Dollar

The preeminent position of sterling as an international currency came to an end with World War I, concurrent with the emergence of the dollar as a rival world currency. Before 1914 the greater part

[4] See Herbert Feis, *Europe: The World's Banker 1870–1914* (New Haven: Yale University Press, 1930).

[5] Britain suspended gold convertibility of sterling at the beginning of World War I and sterling fluctuated in relationship to both gold and the dollar until the pound was stabilized in 1925. In 1931, the relationship between the pound and gold and gold convertible currencies was again broken and sterling fluctuated in relationship to the dollar and other currencies until the outbreak of World War II in 1939, when Britain adopted exchange controls limiting the convertibility of sterling by both residents and nonresidents. Except for a few weeks in 1947 nonresident convertibility of sterling was not fully restored until 1959.

of U.S. trade was financed in London; even the trade between the United States and Latin America was financed by bills on London banks. Following World War I, the dollar developed as the dominant currency in world trade and finance, partly as a consequence of the establishment of the New York acceptance market and other financial institutions equipped to handle international transactions, and partly as a consequence of the large flow of dollar loans and investments to foreign countries. Among the currencies of the major powers, the dollar alone emerged from World War I as a strong and stable currency. The role of world banker shifted from Europe to the United States, which became the leading trader and financial power.

The growing importance of dollar financing in world trade led to a sharp rise in foreign holdings of short-term funds in the United States from about $400 million in July 1921 to more than $3 billion at the end of 1929.[6] This rise in the foreign holdings of dollar funds reflected in part the need for dollar balances to finance trade and to meet service obligations on U.S. foreign loans, and in part the increasing tendency of foreign countries to hold their official reserves in the form of dollars. As stated by the 1943 Department of Commerce study, *The United States in the World Economy*,

> These holdings were largely connected with the development of the gold-exchange standard under which monetary reserves were held partly or wholly in the form of claims on gold-standard countries rather than in gold and which was widely encouraged in the early post-war years as a means of reducing the monetary demand for gold.[7]

During the worldwide depression of the 1930's, foreign short-term assets in the United States declined sharply but rose again to $3.3 billion in 1939. After World War II they rose rapidly. By the end of 1967, foreign holdings of liquid dollar assets totaled $33 billion, nearly half of which represented official reserves of foreign governments and central banks.[8]

---

[6] Hal B. Lary and Associates, *The United States in the World Economy* (Washington, D.C.: U.S. Department of Commerce, 1943), pp. 111–112.

[7] *Ibid.*, p. 115.

[8] Foreign liquid dollar assets include private dollar liabilities to foreigners with a maturity of less than one year plus foreign holdings of U.S. government obligations.

The Role of the Key Currencies

A fundamental characteristic of the modern international payments system is the adoption by the world economic community of a few currencies which serve as the payments media for the vast bulk of international trade and capital transactions. These currencies are referred to as "key currencies," or sometimes as international "reserve currencies," or as "vehicle currencies." These currencies came to be demanded for purposes of holding international liquidity in much the same way that domestic currencies are demanded for holding domestic liquidity. Each trading country could, of course, finance its trade with every other country with its own or perhaps the partner country's currency, and in addition it could hold minimum working balances in the currencies of the countries with which it traded. Instead, however, countries prefer to finance the vast bulk of their international transactions with no more than two currencies and to hold a portion of their international liquid reserves in one or more of these currencies together with gold. The preference for employing only a few currencies in conducting international transactions has risen because of the institutional arrangements and relationships developed in the countries whose currencies have been selected. As has been noted, these include not only the institutions for financing current trade but also a variety of international capital markets which exist in the key currency countries.

It is more convenient and economical for countries to finance their international trade with one or two currencies rather than with many. For a time following World War II, much of the trade between countries outside the dollar area (mainly the United States, Canada, and northern Latin America) was conducted under bilateral payments agreements requiring trade between any two countries to be financed by the currency of one or the other trading partner. But this was an awkward system: first, because it required bilateral balancing of trade over time, and second, because it required the holding of larger operating balances than would have been needed if trade were conducted in only one or two currencies. Traders holding balances sufficient to balance income and expenditure streams in a number of currencies will require larger balances than they would if the separate income and expenditure streams were pooled by conducting all of their trade in one currency.[9]

Not only do traders require balances in the currencies employed in financing trade but, more importantly, the banks that handle the transactions of traders require inventories of these currencies. Since banks desire to minimize their inventories of noninterest-bearing balances, they may find it advantageous to hold interest-bearing assets in the countries whose currencies they have acquired but which they expect to need in the near future. This requires a well-developed money market in the country whose currency is held—something which exists only in the industrially advanced countries of the world. Moreover, there may at times be a net interest differential in favor of holding assets abroad after allowing for the cost of hedging against a decline in the value of the foreign currency. As will be discussed later on, a well-developed forward exchange market is important for reducing the cost of risk avoidance through hedging.

The principal currencies employed in international transactions provide a suitable international liquidity reserve for governments and central banks. Not only may reserves held in the form of foreign obligations earn interest, but the holders avoid the cost of converting foreign exchange into and out of gold which itself involves some cost to hold. Governments and central banks prefer to hold reserves in the form of marketable interest-bearing assets in countries with well-developed financial markets which provide a variety of maturities and interest rates, and which have ample depth and stability. Governments also often prefer to hold currency reserves in countries to which their residents, including the government, are heavily indebted, so that the currency of a large international lender country becomes attractive as a reserve currency. Finally, governments prefer to hold international liquidity reserves in countries whose currencies are expected to remain stable in rela-

---

[9] For a good discussion of this point see Alexander K. Swoboda, *The Euro-Dollar Market: An Interpretation*, Essays in International Finance, No. 64 (Princeton, N.J.: International Finance Section, Princeton University, February 1968), pp. 7–9.

tion to their own domestic currency. Stability in relation to the currency of the reserve asset holder is especially important to avoid an erosion of the domestic currency value of the reserve assets. Hence, countries have been known to be quite willing to hold reserves in a currency to which their own currency may be pegged as a consequence of close trading and financial ties, even though the reserve currency may be fluctuating in relation to third currencies.

The preferred currencies today are the dollar and the pound, and to a lesser extent the French franc by reason of France's close trading and financial ties with the former French dependencies that make up the French franc area. The currencies of some countries are frequently used in foreign transactions but only when those countries are involved in the transaction. Thus, the Canadian dollar is sometimes employed in certain transactions with the United States or with members of the sterling area; the Dutch guilder, the Belgian franc, and the Swedish kroner are sometimes used in transactions involving these countries as one of the trading partners. However, the degree to which a currency plays a key currency role is measured by the extent to which it is used in financing transactions between countries other than the key currency country itself. In this sense the dollar and the pound, in that order, are the predominant key currencies of the world.

The development of the key currency role, then, is partly a matter of historical accident, partly a matter of the development of the necessary institutional framework and worldwide trade and financial relationships, and partly a matter of the economic strength and the economic and political stability of the country concerned. All of these factors were important in the development of the pound and the dollar as key currencies. It should be emphasized, however, that economic strength and financial stability are not sufficient in themselves. For example, Germany is the second largest international trading country in the world and has a strong balance of payments and a high gold reserve ratio. Nevertheless, the Deutsche mark has not become a key currency, nor do other countries hold large official reserves in Deutsche marks. Indeed, Germany has not sought a key currency role, as evidenced by its restrictions on the payment of interest on nonresident balances and on foreign holdings of fixed interest-bearing securities. Although there has been a marked decline in the use of sterling as a trading currency,[10] there is no evidence that sterling's place as the second most important international currency has been shifted to a third key currency. Nor is there evidence that the weakness in the U.S. balance of payments position during the 1960's has reduced the role of the dollar as a key currency. On the contrary, the growth of the Eurodollar market in financing international transactions and serving as a means of holding international liquidity indicates an enlargement of the international role of the dollar.

The Eurodollar Market

The worldwide use of the U.S. dollar has been considerably expanded in recent years by the development of the Eurodollar market and by the practice of issuing bonds denominated in Eurodollars outside the United States. Eurodollars originate with a deposit of dollars in a European bank (frequently a European branch of an American bank). Usually the depositor receives a time deposit in dollars and the bank receives title to a dollar demand deposit in a U.S. bank. Once created, the typical Eurodollar dollar deposit goes through a chain of lending and redepositing. This process may be illustrated as follows:[11]

(1) The ABC Corporation of Europe transfers $1 million which it has on deposit in a bank in the United States to the branch of an American bank in London. The deposit in the American branch constitutes a Eurodollar deposit. The deposit in the bank in the United States is now owned by the American branch in London.

(2) The London branch of the American bank redeposits the million dollars in the form of a time deposit with a bank in Belgium. This transfers ownership of the dollar deposit in the United States from the American branch bank to the Belgian bank. The original deposit is still a liability of the U.S. banking system, but now there are two European dollar liabilities—that of the London branch to the ABC Corporation and that of the Belgian bank to

---

[10] See Paul Einzig, "The Declining Use of Sterling as a Trading Currency," *Westminster Bank Review*, May 1968, pp. 2–10.

[11] Based on a similar illustration in *Euro-Dollar Financing* (New York: The Chase Manhattan Bank, 1968), pp. 13–15.

the London branch of the American bank—based on one deposit in the United States.

(3) The Belgian bank lends the dollars—i.e., the deposit in the United States—to a Belgian importer who makes a dollar payment to a Swiss exporter, who then purchases Eurobonds for his personal portfolio. The latter transaction shifts the deposit to a multinational company issuing the Eurobonds, which in turn deposits the proceeds temporarily as a Eurodollar deposit in an American branch bank in Paris.

(4) A bank in the United States borrows the dollars from the American branch bank in Paris.

There are several advantages in using Eurodollar deposits over direct dollar deposits in a U.S. bank. Foreign depositors can deal directly with their own bank rather than with an American bank. Eurodollar depositors may earn a higher interest in Europe than in the United States, and in many cases it is cheaper for a European to borrow Eurodollars in Europe where he is well known than it is for him to borrow dollars in the United States. The bank in which the Eurodollar deposits are made may lend the Eurodollars at interest or purchase securities with them; it may lend dollars or it may convert the dollars into another currency and lend that currency. It may even deposit Eurodollars with other banks that pay a rate of interest higher than that paid to its own depositors. It is estimated that some $20 billion in Eurodollar deposits are in circulation outside the United States.[12]

U.S. commercial banks also borrow from the Eurodollar market, mainly through their overseas branches. As of June 1968, U.S. banks had liabilities to their overseas branches in excess of $6 billion. Most of these funds represented Eurodollar deposits with the overseas branches of American banks.[13]

[12] For a description of the Eurodollar market see Oscar L. Altman, "Recent Developments in Foreign Markets for Dollars and Other Currencies," IMF *Staff Papers*, X (1963), 48–96; and "Eurodollars: Some Further Comments," IMF *Staff Papers*, XII (1965), 1–16; see also *Euro-Dollar Financing*, p. 25; and "Sustained Expansion in Eurodollar Banking," *Monthly Economic Letter* (New York: First National City Bank of New York, October 1968), pp. 116–119.

[13] See Fred H. Klopstock, "Euro-Dollars and the Liquidity and Reserve Management of United States Banks," *Monthly Review* (New York: Federal Reserve Bank of New York, July 1968), p. 130.

Eurodollars are also used in financing the flotation and purchase of dollar bonds issued overseas (Eurobonds). European and foreign firms operating in Europe find it desirable to issue securities in the European capital markets. American firms operating in Europe have been borrowing large amounts of funds in the European capital markets, especially since the imposition of restrictions by the U.S. government on capital outflow to Europe. Multinational firms generally prefer to borrow dollars because such funds are accepted throughout the world and can be used free of exchange or capital controls in conducting worldwide operations. At the same time, international investors prefer dollar-denominated bonds, and Eurobond financing in dollars has tended to be less expensive than borrowing in other currencies. While some Eurobonds have been denominated in Deutsche marks or in Swiss francs, Eurobond issues denominated in dollars accounted for 76 percent of all such issues in 1966 and 91 percent in 1967.[14] An estimated $2 billion in bonds denominated in Eurodollars was issued in 1967, and a larger amount is expected to be issued in 1968.

Financing Goods and Services

It is customary to divide international transactions into two categories: (1) the flow of goods and services and (2) capital transactions. The financing of goods and services gives rise to capital movements, but there are many capital transactions that are unrelated to the movement of goods and services. This is true, for example, of the purchase of securities by a resident of one country from a resident of another. Exports of goods and services may be financed in a variety of ways, and this financing may or may not involve a foreign exchange transaction. A foreign exchange transaction occurs when there is a transfer of a currency or a claim on a currency which is not the currency of one of the partners to the transfer. For example, a resident of the United States may transfer a dollar deposit to an Englishman in payment for imports from Britain, and the Englishman may transfer the dollar deposit to his

---

[14] *Euro-Dollar Financing*, p. 24.

bank in exchange for pounds. Thus, a foreign exchange transaction involves the transferring of purchasing power from one currency into another. (By "currency" we mean the national money as defined, usually demand deposits in banks plus legal tender currency.) A claim on a currency may take the form of a bill of exchange drawn on the buyer (or his bank)[15] by the seller and payable on presentation (sight), or the claim may be payable at a stated time in the future, say in three months.

Exports of goods and services that do not give rise in the first instance to a foreign exchange transaction include those made available under long-term credit arrangements, or as government grants or private gifts; goods sold under open account or on consignment; and exports of goods and services by a firm in one country to its branch or an affiliate in another country.[16] Such transactions do not have a *direct* effect on the foreign exchange market since the importer need not acquire the currency of the seller (or draw on his inventory of the seller's currency) or increase the supply of his own currency in the hands of a nonresident in case payment is made with the buyer's currency. However, long-term credit transactions, or even gifts in kind, may have an indirect effect on the foreign exchange market, since the credits (or gifts) may be used to import goods that would have otherwise been acquired by a foreign exchange transaction. Exports of goods and services by a

[15] A substantial amount of trade is financed by means of letters of credit issued by the bank of the importer (or by the foreign correspondent of the importer's bank). The letter of credit authorizes the exporter to draw drafts in his own or a foreign currency on the bank issuing the letter of credit. If the letter of credit calls for payment at some stated time in the future, the issuing bank writes "accepted" on the face of the draft drawn by the seller, and payment is made when the banker's acceptance comes due. Meanwhile, it may be sold in the acceptance market or held by the seller until it is due. The accepting bank will look to the foreign buyer or his bank for delivery of the currency called for by the letter of credit at the time the acceptance becomes due.

[16] Foreign aid in the form of loans or grants may also involve a foreign exchange transaction. The donor agency may make available funds (or guarantee a bank letter of credit) to the aid recipient which may be used for purchases of specific commodities or services or, in some cases, for any purpose. Thereafter, normal foreign exchange transactions may take place between the actual exporters and importers of the goods and services financed by the foreign aid.

firm to its foreign affiliate may also have an indirect effect upon the foreign exchange market. For example, if a firm invests abroad by shipping machinery to its affiliate[17] which enables the affiliate to increase its earnings abroad, those earnings may eventually be returned to the parent company in the form of dividends through the foreign exchange market. Also, long-term credits must eventually be repaid with interest, and this increases the foreign exchange receipts of the lender country. It should be noted that a very substantial proportion of total trade is financed by means which do not involve a direct foreign exchange transaction. A high proportion of commercial exports are shipped under credit terms ranging from three to five years or more; and it has been estimated that some 25 percent of U.S. exports of manufactured goods represents shipments from American firms to their branches or affiliates abroad.[18]

Capital transactions unrelated to the financing of goods and services may serve indirectly to finance current trade. Suppose an American bank purchases securities issued by a foreign firm or government and pays for the securities by the transfer of dollar deposits to the issuer. The immediate effect is to increase the supply of U.S. dollars in the hands of the foreign borrower. The borrower may use the additional dollars (foreign exchange) to expand purchases of goods and services in the United States; he may sell the dollars in the foreign exchange market for his own currency or for a third currency; he may hold the dollars for a time to supplement his working balance; or he may sell them to the central bank in his own country, which may hold the dollars as a part of its international reserves. A rise in the reserves of the central bank or government of the borrower may lead that government to liberalize its import restrictions and permit its residents to buy more from abroad. However, the increase in the supply of dollars in the hands of foreigners will not necessarily lead to an expansion of U.S. exports. The dollars may simply be sold on the foreign exchange

---

[17] The parent firm acquires a claim on its affiliate through the shipment of machinery, thereby making a long-term investment which, in the balance of payments, is offset by the machinery exports.

[18] Samuel Pizer and Frederick Cutler, "U.S. Exports to Foreign Affiliates of U.S. Firms," *Survey of Current Business*, December 1965, pp. 12–16.

market and, if the additional supply of dollars is not matched by an additional demand, the price of the dollar in terms of other currencies will tend to fall.

The Foreign Exchange Market

We have noted two functions of the foreign exchange market: the transfer of purchasing power from one national currency into another; and the advancing of short- and medium-term credit.[19] A third function performed by the foreign exchange market is that of enabling holders of foreign currencies or claims on foreign currencies, and traders with future obligations in foreign currencies, to avoid the risk of loss arising from a change in the rate of exchange. This third or hedging function is performed by the forward exchange market in which traders make contracts with banks to sell or acquire a foreign currency at a specified time in the future at a pre-agreed price in terms of their own currency. Thus, if an American importer has an obligation to pay in sterling three months from now for some wool which he has purchased from a British exporter, he wants to be sure what the sterling will cost him when this obligation becomes due. The importer could immediately buy the sterling he needs at the spot rate of, say, $2.40 per pound sterling and hold it until his obligation becomes due. But this ties up the importer's funds, and he may have other, more immediate, uses for his

[19] Nearly all foreign trade transactions involve credit, an exception being the case in which the seller demands payment in advance of shipment. Even a sight bill of exchange drawn by the seller on the buyer or his bank involves credit during the short period required to transmit the bill and make payment in the currency called for, perhaps by means of a cable transfer of a bank deposit. Time drafts may be drawn on either the importer or his bank (in response to a letter of credit), which may call for payment up to a year or even more after shipment is made. Such transactions involve the use of foreign exchange instruments; since the exporter usually discounts the time draft with his bank, there is a direct effect on the foreign exchange market by virtue of the increase in the supply of claims on a foreign currency held by the exporter's bank. In contrast, medium- or long-term commercial credits represented by notes given to the exporter by the importer or by sales on open account do not have a *direct* impact on the foreign exchange market. Such claims, however, might induce the exporter to hedge by selling the foreign currency in the forward exchange market.

money. However, he can make a contract with his bank for sterling to be delivered three months hence at, say, $2.404.

At the same time, there will be American exporters who have contracted to receive sterling three months hence in payment for goods shipped abroad, and who need to know in advance what they can obtain for this sterling when they receive it. The exporters can contract with their bank to sell the sterling which they will receive in three months at a price of, say, $2.399. Regardless of what happens to the price of sterling in the spot market three months hence, settlements will be made according to the terms of the forward contracts, and, for a relatively small cost, both traders will have avoided the risk of an adverse change in the current spot rate of $2.40. The bank can make a profit from the difference between the forward buying rate and the forward selling rate, and if the bank has purchased and sold equal amounts of sterling three months forward, the bank will not have incurred any risk either. However, the rates on forward sterling will depend upon demand and supply as determined by the requirements of traders who want to avoid risk and by the expectations of bankers and speculators who are willing to take a long or short position in forward sterling. There will also be traders in other countries who have obligations to make dollar payments in the future or who hold claims on dollars payable in the future and who, therefore, want to avoid the risk of a change in the price of the dollar in terms of their own currencies. They will also be led to make contracts with their banks for the purchase or sale of forward dollars.

Thus, we see that the markets for foreign exchange involve trading in claims on foreign currencies payable immediately (the spot market) and at various dates in the future (the forward market). Foreign exchange markets exist in all of the major financial centers of the world, and the principal foreign currencies traded are the key currencies against one another or against the domestic (non-key) currency of the country in which the market is located. A full description of the organization and operation of these markets is beyond the scope of this book. But it should be noted that all of the major markets are closely integrated, so that at any point in time the price of sterling in terms of dollars in the New York market is consistent with the price of the dollar in terms of shillings and pence in the London market; and the price of sterling in terms of Canadian dollars in Montreal is consistent with the price of sterling and of Canadian dollars in New York in terms of U.S. dollars.[20] Banks and foreign exchange brokers as well as foreign exchange speculators operating in the spot and forward exchange markets undertake arbitrage transactions in two or more markets in order to keep the crossrates on the various currencies consistent.[21] In analyzing the demand for and the supply of a currency in the foreign exchange markets, we must keep in mind that shifts in demand-and-supply forces in one market are transmitted to all markets in which the currencies are traded, and that operations in different markets are symmetrical. Thus, an increase in the demand for sterling in terms of dollars in the New York market has the same effect on the dollar-sterling rate as an increase in the supply of dollars in the London market, and the resulting change in the dollar-sterling rate will also affect the U.S. dollar-French franc rate, the sterling-Canadian dollar rate, or the Canadian dollar-U.S. dollar rate.

The Demand for and Supply of Dollars

Let us now consider the sources of demand and supply for U.S. dollars. One source of supply of dollars arises when an American importer pays dollars to a foreign exporter. The exporter will normally sell the dollars to his bank, which in turn may hold the dollars in order to build up its balances in the United States; alternatively the bank may use the dollars to purchase American interest-bearing assets; or it may sell the dollars either in the foreign exchange market or to its central bank. The central bank may, in turn, hold the dollars as an addition to its international liquidity reserves, sell the dollars in the foreign exchange market

[20] For an excellent discussion of the operation of foreign exchange markets see Allan R. Holmes and Francis H. Schott, *The New York Foreign Exchange Market* (New York: Federal Reserve Bank of New York, 1965).

[21] If the pound sterling is selling at $2.40 in New York and the French franc at $.20, then the pound should be selling at 12 francs in the Paris exchange. If the pound were selling at, say, 11.5 francs, the crossrate between the dollar and sterling is said to be broken or the crossrates are inconsistent.

for its own or a third currency, or present the dollars to the U.S. Treasury for conversion into gold. Sales of dollars in the foreign exchange market tend to depress the price of dollars in terms of other currencies. Purchases by Americans of foreign capital assets with dollars also increase the supply of dollars, which may or may not be sold in the foreign exchange markets, depending upon the desire of the recipients. American tourists spending dollars abroad will also increase the supply of dollars. Americans may also acquire foreign currencies in the foreign exchange market with dollars, with a resulting increase in the supply of dollars in the hands of foreigners, or the foreign currencies may be acquired from other American residents who happen to hold foreign currency. These actions will tend to raise the price of foreign currencies in terms of the dollar or, conversely, depress the price of the dollar in terms of the foreign currencies. However, an increase in the supply of dollars in the hands of foreigners will not necessarily have a direct impact on the foreign exchange market, since foreigners acquiring the dollars may simply decide to hold more dollars.

A demand for dollars occurs when foreigners require dollars to make payments either to the United States or to third countries for goods and services or for capital assets. The foreigners may use some of their accumulated dollars to make dollar payments rather than acquire additional dollars in the foreign exchange market. The fact that foreigners are willing to hold more dollars than they require for immediate payments or for minimum operating balances means that there can be substantial changes in the supply of dollars relative to the demand for current dollar payments without substantially affecting the value of the dollar in terms of foreign currencies. This is an important characteristic of an international reserve currency. The role of the central bank is especially significant here since central banks tend to have an almost infinitely elastic demand for reserves; and if they choose to hold reserves in the form of dollars, they may add to their dollar holdings far beyond their needs for operating balances in this currency.

The Role of Interest Rates
in Capital Movements

The dollar and other currencies are demanded for the purchase of capital assets in foreign countries, and interest differentials between countries play an important role in determining the volume and direction of international capital movements. When interest rates rise in London relative to those in New York, there will be a tendency for banks and other financial institutions in New York to shift short-term funds to London. However, U.S. investors want to avoid the risk of a decline in the value of sterling since even a modest depreciation of sterling would result in a loss in terms of dollars several times the potential gain represented by the difference in interest rates in the two countries. The investors will, therefore, contract to deliver sterling against dollars at an agreed price (the forward rate on sterling), say, three months in the future at the same time that they purchase spot sterling for an investment in British securities which will mature in three months. So long as the cost of hedging—the difference between the forward sterling rate and the spot rate—is less than the interest differential between New York and London, there will be an advantage in moving funds to London.

Let us assume that the rate of interest on three-month government securities is 3 percent per annum in New York and 6 percent per annum in London. If the spot price of sterling is \$2.40 and the forward price of sterling is \$2.39, the interest differential in favor of three-month sterling securities (three-fourths of 1 percent for three months) is larger than the cost of hedging (four-tenths of 1 percent), which is the difference between the spot and forward prices of sterling expressed as a percentage of the spot rate. In fact, there will be an incentive to shift funds to London up to the point where the interest differential just equals the difference between the spot and the forward rate (discount on sterling) expressed in percentage terms. The forward exchange rate is therefore said to be at "interest rate parity" when the interest differential and the forward discount or premium over the spot rate (expressed as a percentage of the spot rate) are equal. Interest arbitrage operations —borrowing in one country and lending in another—have the effect of raising the spot rate on the currency of the country toward which capital is flowing (usually the higher interest rate country)[22] and of depressing the forward rate, thereby increasing the forward discount. On the other hand, interest arbitrage operations tend to reduce the interest differential between the two countries. These two actions tend to equate the interest differential with the spread between the spot and the forward exchange rates (expressed as a percentage of the spot rate).

Presumably, if interest arbitrage operations were unimpeded and there were no government interventions in either the money markets or the foreign exchange markets, such operations would eventually bring about interest rate parity and a cessation of the capital movement induced by the original interest differential. However, governments do intervene in both their money markets and in the foreign exchange markets. Moreover, there may be uncovered capital movements undertaken by traders who elect to take the risk of interest arbitrage without hedging via the forward exchange market. Finally, banks which supply most of the capital for interest arbitrage transactions may not have sufficient funds to devote to this purpose to the extent necessary to achieve interest rate parity. Hence, interest parity is frequently not achieved by market forces.

Because short-term capital movements affect the demand and supply for a country's currency and hence its balance of payments, governments may deliberately intervene in either the money market or the foreign exchange market, or both, for the purpose of influencing capital movements. One method is to raise short-term capital interest rates in the domestic market to attract foreign capital or to keep foreign and domestic capital from flowing out of the country. Since changes in short-term rates are regarded as having a less restrictive impact on the domestic economy than movements of long-term rates, the Federal Reserve authorities several years ago sought to raise short-term rates in the U.S. market

[22] The relationship between the spot and forward rates might be such as to favor a flow of capital to the country with the lower interest rate.

while holding down long-term rates. This maneuver was called "operation twist." In 1963, this policy was supplemented by the Interest Equalization Tax (IET), which taxes American purchasers of foreign securities in order to equalize to the foreigner the cost of borrowing in the United States and abroad. Another method of stemming the outflow of short-term capital is the manipulation of the forward exchange rate. This method has been employed in recent years by British authorities. By keeping the forward discount on sterling low, foreign investors were encouraged to hold British securities on which rates were somewhat higher than those in the United States and in certain other countries, since the smaller the forward discount on sterling the lower the cost of hedging against the possibility of sterling depreciation.[23]

Aside from short-term capital movements, there are other types of capital movements that respond to changes in interest rates and to the outlook for prices in the stock market. Long-term capital movements are usually not hedged, but such movements reflect judgments with respect to the likelihood of devaluation as well as opportunities for differential gains in rates of return (including capital gains) as between countries. Purchases and sales of U.S. long-term securities by foreigners play an important role in the U.S. balance of payments. Most long-term foreign debt obligations acquired by Americans are denominated in dollars so that there is no risk of a change in the exchange rate for the American investors, but there is a risk for the foreign borrowers. However, the level of long-term interest rates in the United States as compared with rates abroad determines the attractiveness to foreigners of borrowing in the U.S. market.

The Par Value System and the Role of Gold

All free-world industrialized countries (with the notable exception of Switzerland) and most developing countries are mem-

[23] For a good discussion of the pros and cons of this technique see Henry N. Goldstein, "Further Thoughts on Official Support of the Forward Exchange Rate," *Quarterly Journal of Economics*, August 1966, pp. 443–455.

bers of the International Monetary Fund (IMF). The Articles of Agreement of the IMF set forth certain ground rules for the international payments system, one of the most important of which is the system of gold parities under which each member of the Fund (with a few exceptions) has defined the par value of its currency in terms of gold. Each member is required to maintain the value of its currency in terms of other member currencies within a range of 1 percent above and below parity. (With each currency defined in terms of gold, it is easy to calculate the exchange parity of each currency in terms of every other currency.) In practice, this is accomplished by each country intervening in the foreign exchange market to prevent the price of its currency from deviating from parity by more than 1 percent in relation to one of the key currencies (usually the dollar). In the case of the United States, parity is maintained by the willingness of the U.S. Treasury Department to sell gold at a fixed price at $35 per ounce against dollars offered by foreign monetary authorities (central banks and treasuries). However, during the past several years the U.S. monetary authorities have also supported the dollar in the exchange markets with foreign currencies. Members of the IMF also agreed to consult with the Fund (and in some cases obtain its permission) before changing their gold parities. Finally, all of the major industrial countries have accepted the obligation of the Fund Agreement to maintain convertibility of their currencies into one another in the sense that nonresident holders of a currency are free to sell that currency in the foreign exchange markets of the world in exchange for their own or a third currency.

The role of gold in the modern international payments system is often misunderstood, and even international financial experts differ on the significance and essentiality of gold for an efficient payments system. Gold is one of the assets employed as an international reserve by governments or central banks. The other reserve assets include reserve currencies and automatic drawing rights in the IMF. As of December 31, 1967, gold represented $40 billion out of total official reserves of $73 billion. Gold does not serve as a regulator of the volume of domestic currency and has not played this role since before World War I; even during the nineteenth century, gold controlled the volume of domestic currency only to a limited extent. While par values of currencies are defined in terms of gold under the IMF system, this standard is not indispensable; par values could be defined in terms of units of a reserve currency or conceivably in terms of a composite of currencies.[24]

Under the present system, the link between gold and the world's major currencies is established two ways. First, the U.S. government stands ready to sell gold against dollars offered by foreign monetary authorities at a fixed price of $35 per ounce. No other government has committed itself to sell gold at a fixed price. Second, members of the IMF are obligated, under the terms of the Articles of Agreement, to buy gold against their own currencies at the official price in terms of the gold parity of their currency when such gold is offered by the IMF. The *gold exchange standard*, which is the name given to the present international monetary system, derives its character from these two conditions. However, the IMF par value system could still exist if the first condition— namely, the willingness of the United States to sell gold to monetary authorities at a fixed price—were terminated. In fact, nothing in the Articles of Agreement requires the United States to continue this practice. The exchange parities between national currencies could be maintained by the second condition alone. Countries would be obligated to maintain their exchange rates within 1 percent of the established par value by supporting the value of their currency in the foreign exchange markets. They can exchange their gold for the foreign currencies needed for this purpose through the IMF, and the IMF, in turn, can replenish its supply of the currencies demanded by selling gold.[25] However, a country does not need to hold gold to support the value of its currency in the foreign exchange market. It can hold its reserves in the form

---

[24] The Articles of Agreement of the IMF stipulate that the par value of a member's currency may be expressed either in terms of gold or in terms of the U.S. dollar of the weight and fineness in effect on July 1, 1944. (Article IV, Section 1 (a).) The Articles of Agreement of the IMF has been published by all member governments and by the IMF.

[25] In mid-1968, a controversy arose over whether the South African government could sell gold acquired from its mines to the IMF. (See Chapter 5.) However, this is a special case.

of (1) other convertible currencies, or (2) reserve positions in the IMF, or (3), in the future, in the proposed new reserve facility of the Fund called Special Drawing Rights, all of which may be exchanged for convertible currencies. Thus, other reserve assets could be substituted for gold in the maintenance and operation of the par value system.

To summarize, gold serves as a means of defining currency values and as a reserve medium convertible into foreign currencies at a fixed price determined by established gold parities. As we shall see later on, gold has serious weaknesses as an international reserve medium, and an efficient international payment mechanism could be established without gold or any other reserve commodity.

The World Banker Functions of Key Currency Countries

Mention has been made of the institutional basis for the establishment of a key currency which serves both as a vehicle currency in international transactions and as a medium for holding private and official international liquidity. Out of the operations of the financial institutions and of the international capital and commodity markets found in a key currency country, there arise certain world banker functions. These functions are analogous to the role of a commercial bank operating in a domestic community. The central function of a commercial bank is to accept short-term deposits which constitute the money supply of the community and to make loans to private firms and investments in corporate and government securities. In the process of making loans and investments, additional demand deposits (money supply) are created. Similarly, a key currency country receives into its banks and other financial institutions and capital markets funds from all over the world, and, in turn, capital in the form of loans and direct investments flows from the key currency country to the rest of the world. But the obligations of the key currency country to the rest of the world have a special quality. Whether held in the form of demand deposits or in less liquid forms, such as time deposits and securities, these obligations constitute claims on generally accepted means of international payment, and are a preferred medium for holding international liquidity both by the private financial community and by governments and central banks. Equally important, the capital markets of the key currency country provide a source of investment funds for the rest of the world. The fact that the key currency country tends to be a large creditor to the world and that these credits must be serviced in the key currency enhances the desire of foreigners to hold claims on its currency. The proper performance of this function requires broad and diversified markets oriented to international lending and investment and freedom from capital controls which limit the outflow or the inflow of capital. Thus, the key currency country performs a kind of inter-mediation function for the world, importing capital from the rest of the world and supplying the world's needs for a variety of types of capital, including both loans and direct investments.

But why doesn't the rest of the world supply its own capital requirements from its own sources of capital funds? For example, why doesn't Europe, which claims that it no longer needs net capital imports from the United States, supply its capital needs directly from its own savings? Professor Charles P. Kindleberger answers this question by stating that Europeans have a greater preference for liquid assets than Americans and that Europeans prefer to hold relatively short-term assets while the United States supplies Europe's need for long-term investment capital which is not met by European savers.[26] Perhaps the best explanation of the inter-

[26] C. P. Kindleberger, *Balance of Payments Deficits and the International Market for Liquidity*, Essays in International Finance, No. 46 (Princeton, N.J.: International Finance Section, Princeton University, May 1965.) Robert Triffin has challenged Kindleberger's thesis by showing that U.S. long-term investments in Europe are roughly balanced by Europe's long-term investments in the United States (as of 1965) and that, in addition, private short-term European holdings in the United States are less than 25 percent of total private American investments in Europe. (*The Balance of Payments and the Foreign Investment Position of the United States*, Essays in International Finance, No. 55 [Princeton, N.J.: International Finance Section, Princeton University, September 1966], pp. 10–12.) Kindleberger has replied to Triffin by suggesting that Europeans invest in the United States a portion of the dollars they receive from the spending in Europe of U.S. loans to less developed countries as well as from U.S. dollar investments in Europe. Such investments, whether long-term or short-term, are made because of the liquidity

mediation function is to be found in the structure of the capital markets and financial intermediaries in the United States as compared with that in Europe and in the rest of the world. U.S. capital markets and financial intermediaries are able to provide savers with a high degree of liquidity while these same institutions hold the bulk of their assets in nonliquid loans and investments. These loans and investments supply a variety of capital requirements throughout the world. In addition, much of the world has a strong preference for holding claims on an international currency over claims on their own currency. The intermediation function is discussed further in subsequent chapters.

Before World War I, Britain was a large net capital exporter, but this has not been true in recent years. However, the process of intermediation has continued in Britain, particularly in its relations with the sterling area. Indeed, one of the principal arguments for continued membership in the sterling area and for holding currency reserves in sterling has been the opportunity of the outer sterling area to obtain long-term financing in the London market. Thus, the outer sterling area is both a large debtor to and a creditor of London. But the current weakness of sterling and the sterling devaluation of 1967 have reduced the willingness of the outer sterling area countries to hold their reserves in sterling,[27] and British capital controls during the post-World War II period impaired Britain's intermediation function. Similarly, both the reduced confidence in the dollar and the controls on capital exports imposed by the U.S. government, beginning with the Interest Equalization Tax in 1963, have impaired the world banker functions of the United States.[28] It is the view of the author that the world banker functions of key currency countries may be more important than the official reserve medium function of key cur-

---

afforded by broad markets in the United States, while Europeans borrow from the United States and from the Eurodollar market to obtain relatively cheap credit. (C. P. Kindleberger, "The Pros and Cons of an International Capital Market," *Zeitschrift für die Gesamte Staatswissenschaft*, October 1967, pp. 600–617.)

[27] See "Sterling Area's End," *The Wall Street Journal*, June 24, 1968, p. 1.

[28] See Raymond F. Mikesell, "United States as World Banker," *The National Banking Review*, December 1966, pp. 145–150.

rencies. It is quite possible that nations will, by agreement or otherwise, cease to hold foreign currencies as a part of their official reserves. But in the absence of a breakdown in the international monetary mechanism, key currency countries will continue to provide private or nonofficial international liquidity, and assets denominated in key currencies will continue to have the special qualities indicated above.

2

The Balance of Payments

THE BALANCE OF PAYMENTS is a statistical tabulation of economic transactions between residents of one country and the residents of the rest of the world.[1] The principal categories of economic transactions that appear in the balance of payments are shown in Table 1. Conceptually, the balance of payments tabulation is based on the double entry principle. For each transaction recorded, say the export of a commodity from the United States or the purchase of a U.S. government bond by a foreign bank, there is an entry of an equal amount of the opposite sign implied in the balance of payments statement. Thus, if a merchandise export of $1,000 is paid for by a draft drawn by a foreigner or his bank on the foreigner's bank account in the United States, there are theoretically two entries: (1) $1,000 credit entry under merchandise exports; and (2) $1,000 short-term capital outflow representing the reduction in foreign dollar deposits (a debit entry). Likewise, the purchase by a foreigner of a $1,000 U.S. government bond would usually involve the following entries: (1) $1,000 long-

[1] The term "resident" has a special meaning here since not all "residents," for balance of payments purposes, actually reside in the country whose balance of payments is tabulated. For example, an American army unit stationed in Germany or a U.S. embassy in a foreign country is a resident of the United States for balance of payments purposes; transactions between the U.S. Army unit in Germany and the German economy are considered to be international transactions, while transactions between the United States and the U.S. Army unit abroad are domestic transactions. Likewise, transactions between the United States economy and the United Nations in New York or the World Bank or the British embassy in Washington are regarded as international transactions or transactions with nonresidents of the United States.

term capital inflow (credit); and (2) $1,000 short-term capital outflow (debit).

However, this is not the way the various items in the balance of payments are actually tabulated. It would be impossible to draw up a balance of payments showing the credit and debit entries corresponding to each transaction as in the above illustration. There are millions of transactions and many ways of financing exports or imports or other categories of transactions; information on how each transaction is financed or offset by a transaction of the opposite sign is not available. In the case of merchandise exports, total exports are recorded but the payments arrangements relating to these exports are hidden in figures showing net changes in bank balances and other financial assets of foreigners in the United States and of American assets in foreign countries. Thus, the balance of payments account presents a highly aggregate picture of the transactions of residents with foreigners, since the means of financing goods and services and of transfers of long-term capital assets are reflected only in *net* changes in short-term credit balances over the period under review.

This fact raises a number of problems in the interpretation or analysis of the balance of payments. For example, were the net changes in a country's short-term international assets and liabilities, including gold holdings (usually regarded as a measure of balance of payments surplus or deficit), the result of a change in the merchandise account or of long-term capital movements, and why did these changes come about? The analysis is complicated by the fact that the various categories and transactions are interdependent. Thus, long-term capital exports affect the trade balance by increasing exports, and capital imports may be accompanied by larger merchandise imports.

An oversimplified way of looking at the balance of payments is to calculate the difference between exports and imports of goods and services and to regard the net change in the remaining items— short- and long-term capital movements, unilateral transfers and gold—as financing the current account surplus or deficit. This is a gross oversimplification because the so-called financing transactions, for which only net figures are usually available, are in con-

TABLE 1

U.S. Balance of Payments 1964, 1965, 1966, and 1967

(In millions of dollars)

Item	1964	1965	1966	1967[p]
Exports of Goods and Services—Total[1]	37,099	39,147	43,039	45,693
Merchandise	25,297	26,244	29,168	30,463
Military sales	747	844	847	1,272
Transportation	2,324	2,390	2,589	2,701
Travel	1,207	1,380	1,573	1,641
Investment income receipts, private	4,929	5,376	5,650	6,163
Investment income receipts, govt.	460	512	595	622
Other services	2,135	2,401	2,617	2,831
Imports of Goods and Services—Total	−28,637	−32,203	−37,937	−40,893
Merchandise	−18,621	−21,472	−25,510	−26,980
Military expenditures	−2,861	−2,921	−3,694	−4,319
Transportation	−2,462	−2,674	−2,914	−2,965
Travel	−2,211	−2,438	−2,657	−3,170
Investment income payments	−1,455	−1,729	−2,074	−2,277
Other services	−1,027	−969	−1,088	−1,182
Balance on Goods and Services[2]	8,462	6,944	5,102	4,800
Remittances and Pensions	−896	−1,024	−1,010	−1,284
1. Balance on Goods, Services, Remittances, and Pensions	7,566	5,920	4,092	3,516
2. U.S. Govt. Grants and Capital Flow, Net	−3,560	−3,375	−3,446	−4,127
Grants,[2] loans, and net change in foreign currency holdings, and short-term claims	−4,263	−4,277	−4,680	−5,128
Scheduled repayments on U.S. govt. loans	580	681	806	996
Nonscheduled repayments and selloffs	123	221	428	5

3. U.S. Private Capital Flow, Net	-6,542	-3,743	-4,213	-5,446
Direct investments	-2,435	-3,418	-3,543	-3,027
Foreign securities	-677	-758	-482	-1,252
Other long-term claims:				
Reported by banks	-941	-232	337	284
Reported by others	-343	-88	-112	-301
Short-term claims:				
Reported by banks	-1,523	325	-84	-739
Reported by others	-623	428	-329	-411
4. Foreign Capital Flow, Net Excluding Change in Liquid Assets in U.S.	685	278	2,512	3,077
Long-term investments	109	-68	2,176	2,235
Short-term claims	113	149	269	390
Nonliquid claims on U.S. govt. associated with-military contracts	228	314	341	68
U.S. govt. grants and capital	50	-85	-213	-85
Other specified transactions	208	-25	-12	-1
Other nonconvertible, nonmarketable, medium term U.S. govt. securities[3]	-23	-7	-49	470
5. Errors and Unrecorded Transactions	-949	-415	-302	-595

p Preliminary.
[1] Excludes transfers under military grants.
[2] Excludes military grants.
[3] Includes certificates sold abroad by Export-Import Bank.
NOTE: U.S. Department of Commerce data. Minus sign indicates net payments (debits); absence of sign indicates net receipts (credits).
SOURCE: *Federal Reserve Bulletin*, March and April 1968.

siderable measure autonomous and not undertaken with a view to financing the current account. For example, a loan by a U.S. bank to a European bank has no necessary relationship either to the export of goods from the United States or to the covering of a European current account deficit with the United States. Another related point is that all transactions recorded in the balance of payments are directly or indirectly interdependent. Thus, a reduction in U.S. capital exports will not yield an equivalent reduction in the net outflow of the U.S. dollars since the reduction in capital exports will indirectly affect merchandise exports, short-term capital inflow, and other items in the balance of payments.

What Is a Balance of Payments Deficit or Surplus?

It would seem that nearly every person informed on economic matters should know what is meant by a deficit or surplus in the balance of payments. But economists have been debating for years the question of how balance of payments equilibrium should be defined. Actually, there is no right or wrong definition in an absolute sense. Since the balance of payments account is constructed so that the sum of credit entries is equal to the sum of the debit entries,[2] balance of payments analysis is concerned with the relationships among various items. Any concept of balance of payments deficit or surplus is, hence, arbitrary and depends upon the purpose which the analyst had in mind. Usually, the major policy concern of governments with their balance of payments has to do with how quarter-to-quarter or year-to-year changes in their international transactions affect the ability of the monetary authority to maintain the exchange value of the currency. Thus, monetary authorities are concerned with the changes in the level of monetary reserves and with short-term obligations to foreign countries and international institutions such as the IMF. They are also concerned

---

[2] Actually, the total debit and credit items as determined by the available data rarely balance so that a residual item—errors and omissions—is added to the balance of payments statement with the proper sign in order to make it balance.

with the ability of the country to meet future obligations out of future foreign exchange receipts and reserve asset holdings.

The problem of defining the payments balance is more complicated for a reserve currency country than for a nonreserve currency country. A nonreserve currency country will tend to have only modest short-term obligations to foreigners denominated in its own currency, so that its deficit is usually defined as a decrease in its official reserve holdings plus (or minus) any increase (or decrease) in its short-term foreign currency obligations to foreigners. On the other hand, a reserve currency country like the United States has large obligations to foreigners, the vast bulk of which are dollar obligations. What types of obligations to foreigners should be included? And should the calculation of the balance include changes in private obligations or only those of the monetary authorities— i.e., the Treasury and the Federal Reserve System? There is not even agreement within the U.S. government on these issues. Since the publication in April 1965 of the report of the Review Committee for the Balance of Payments Statistics appointed by the U.S. Bureau of the Budget,[3] the U.S. Department of Commerce, which compiles and publishes the balance of payments statistics of the United States, has been presenting two concepts of balance in its quarterly and annual statements. The concept of balance preferred by the Balance of Payments Division of the Department of Commerce is called the "liquidity" concept, while that recommended by the Bureau of the Budget (Bernstein) Committee is called the "official settlements" concept. Under the Department of Commerce "liquidity" concept, the balance (surplus + or deficit −) for a given period is equal to the arithmetic sum of the following "below the line" items:[4]

[3] *The Balance of Payments Statistics of the United States: A Review and Appraisal, Report of the Review Committee for Balance of Payments Statistics to the Bureau of the Budget* (Washington, D.C.: USGPO, 1965). Since Dr. Edward M. Bernstein was chairman of the Committee preparing this report, it is usually referred to as "the Bernstein Report."

[4] The items listed in the text above and in Table 2 are referred to as "below the line" items in the sense that they are regarded as financing the surplus or deficit arising from the sum of the "above the line" transactions. Each concept of balance provides for a different grouping of all of the categories of transactions which make up the balance of payments as between

(1) Increase (+) or decrease (−) in U.S. official reserve assets (gold, convertible currencies, and IMF gold tranche position).

(2) Decrease (+) or increase (−) in U.S. liquid liabilities to all foreigners. (Liquid liabilities include U.S. bank deposits and other private short-term liabilities and all U.S. government marketable or convertible bonds and notes.)

Under the official settlements concept, the balance (surplus + or deficit −) is equal to the arithmetic sum of the following "below the line" items:

(1) Increase (+) or decrease (−) in U.S. official reserve assets.

(2) Decrease (+) or increase (−) in liquid liabilities to foreign official agencies.

(3) Decrease (+) or increase (−) in certain nonliquid liabilities to foreign official agencies (including nonconvertible, nonmarketable, medium-term U.S. securities).

The U.S. balance for the period 1964–1967 as calculated according to the two concepts is shown in Table 2. Thus, in 1966 the United States had a deficit of $1,357 million according to the liquidity concept, and a surplus of $225 million according to the official settlements concept. However, in 1967 the balance was nearly the same for both concepts: a deficit of $3,575 million under the liquidity concept, and a deficit of $3,398 million under the official settlements concept. The major difference between the two concepts is in the treatment of U.S. liabilities to foreigners. Under the liquidity concept, the change in liquid liabilities to all foreigners, private and official, is placed "below the line." Under the

"above the line" and "below the line" transactions, but the sum of the "above the line" and the "below the line" transactions always equals zero. Thus, in both the liquidity and official settlements concepts the merchandise and services transactions, long-term capital imports and exports, and government grants are all above the line. However, in the official settlements concept, foreign *private* holdings of short-term capital and of U.S. government securities are grouped with the "above the line" transactions, while under the liquidity concept, these transactions are grouped in the "below the line" transactions. For a full discussion, see *The Balance of Payments Statistics of the United States: A Review and Appraisal*, Chapter 9.

TABLE 2

U.S. Balance of Payments on the Liquidity and Official Settlements Bases 1964, 1965, 1966, and 1967

(In millions of dollars)

Item	1964	1965	1966	1967
A. Balance on Liquidity Basis				
(deficit, −)	−2,800	−1,335	−1,357	−3,575
Change in U.S. official reserve assets				
(increase, −)	171	1,222	568	52
Gold	125[1]	1,665	571	1,170
Convertible currencies	−220	−349	−540	−1,024
IMF gold tranche position	266[1]	−94	537	−94
Change in liquid liabilities to all foreign accounts (decrease, −)	2,629	113	789	3,523
Foreign central banks and govts.: Convertible nonmarketable U.S. govt. securities[2]	376	122	−945	455
Marketable U.S. govt. bonds and notes[2]	−58	−20	−245	48
Deposits, short-term U.S. govt. securities, etc.	757	−154	−582	1,547
IMF (gold deposits)	—	34	177	22
Commercial banks abroad	1,454	116	2,697	1,265
Other private residents of foreign countries	343	306	212	394
International and regional organizations other than IMF	−243	−291	−525	−208
B. Balance on Settlements Basis				
(deficit, −)	−1,549	−1,304	225	−3,398
Change in U.S. official reserve assets (increase, −)	171	1,222	568	52
Change in liquid liabilities to foreign central banks and govts. and IMF (see detail above under A).	1,075	−18	−1,595	2,072
Change in certain nonliquid liabilities to foreign central banks and govts.:				
Of U.S. private organizations	149	−38	788	820
Of U.S. govt.	154	138	14	454

[1]Reflects $259-million payment of gold portion of increased U. S. subscription to IMF.
[2]With original maturities over one year.
NOTE: U. S. Department of Commerce data. Minus sign indicates net payments (debits); absence of sign indicates net receipts (credits). Signs reversed on lines A and B.
SOURCE: *Federal Reserve Bulletin*, March and April 1968.

official settlements concept, only changes in liquid liabilities to foreign official agencies are placed "below the line." In addition, under the official settlements concept changes in certain nonliquid liabilities are placed "below the line." These consist mainly of nonmarketable, nonconvertible, medium-term U.S. securities issued by the U.S. government and denominated in foreign currencies,[5] and of certificates of deposit with a maturity of more than one year issued by U.S. banks to foreign central banks.

There are important differences in rationale behind the two concepts of balance outlined above. Under the liquidity concept, it is implicitly assumed that all liquid dollar obligations to foreigners constitute a potential threat to the exchange value of the dollar, and not just those held by foreign monetary authorities. This is true since any foreign holder of dollars may sell his dollars in the foreign exchange market and depress the value of the dollar. But this is also true for all dollars held by American residents so long as they are free to buy foreign currencies. The rationale underlying the official settlements concept is that, since only monetary authorities have the responsibility for maintaining stable exchange rates, balance of payments deficits and surpluses should be measured by changes in the international asset and liability positions of monetary authorities. Also, only foreign monetary authorities can convert dollar holdings into gold at the U.S. Treasury.[6] Moreover, the official settlements concept has the advantage of sym-

---

[5] These nonmarketable, nonconvertible U.S. government securities issued to foreign governments and central banks are denominated in foreign currencies. Hence these obligations do not give rise to an increase in liquid dollar liabilities to foreigners under the liquidity concept of balance. Changes in these obligations are included "below the line" in the official settlements concept. To exclude increases in these obligations in the determination of the U.S. deficit appears to many economists as a form of statistical trickery. Ostensibly the purpose of issuing these securities is to acquire foreign currencies for use in defending the exchange market value of the dollar. However, since some of these securities are issued against dollars, it appears that the purpose of the device may be to induce foreign governments to accept assets denominated in their own currency for dollars, rather than use these dollars to buy gold from the U.S. Treasury.

[6] However, any private foreign resident can buy gold in the free gold markets abroad for dollars, and before March 1968 the United States and the other members of the London gold pool were supplying gold to the London market in order to prevent the price of gold from rising appreciably above $35 an ounce.

metry in that, except for the injection of new monetary reserves into the international monetary system, a deficit in one country is reflected in a surplus in the rest of the world. Under the liquidity concept, a deficit arising from an increase in liquid liabilities to private foreign residents does not result in a surplus in foreign countries since there is no increase in the official reserves of other countries.[7] On the other hand, the proponents of the liquidity concept argue that an increase in U.S. liabilities to private entities abroad may constitute just as great a threat to the foreign exchange value of the dollar as do liabilities to foreign monetary authorities. In fact, the threat may be greater since foreign monetary authorities may be constrained not to sell their dollar holdings in the foreign exchange markets for fear that additional reserve losses by the United States would reduce confidence in the dollar and thereby weaken the entire international monetary structure.

Professor Kindleberger and others have argued that both the liquidity and the official settlements concepts of balance are inadequate because they do not take into account the essential world banker function of the reserve currency country.[8] According to Kindleberger, when the United States accepts bank deposits and incurs other short-term liabilities from foreign countries while simultaneously making long-term loans and direct investments abroad, it is not increasing its deficit but is simply swapping assets in response to differences in liquidity preferences at home and abroad. This is exactly what a commercial bank does when it increases its demand deposits and makes loans, and no one accuses a bank of having a deficit when it expands its loans and deposits. In fact, this is the only way that a bank can grow. It is through this process that a key currency country supplies the additional liquidity (private and official reserve currency balances) that the world requires for a growth in production and trade. This intermediation function of the United States as world banker is weakened when foreign central banks convert their dollar holdings into gold from the U.S. Treasury. Kindleberger argues that the holding

[7] *Balance of Payments Statistics* . . . , pp. 110–111.
[8] C. P. Kindleberger, *Balance of Payments Deficits and the International Market for Liquidity*, Essays in International Finance No. 46 (Princeton, N.J.: International Finance Section, Princeton University, May 1965).

of dollar balances abroad is "a necessary counterpart of the inter-mediation which provides liquidity to Europe's savers and financial institutions."[9] Critics of the Kindleberger position point out that the United States is not an international central bank whose liabilities the rest of the world is willing to hold without limit. Granted that there may be differences in liquidity preferences between European savers and those in the United States, it is pointed out that Europeans desire to hold short-term assets in their own currencies or in gold rather than in the form of dollars. Thus, when U.S. long-term capital flows to Europe and is not accompanied by an increase in U.S. exports relative to imports, Europe accumulates dollars reluctantly in the sense that European central banks acquire the dollars from their residents who desire other assets, but the central banks forego converting their dollar balances into gold so as not to increase the gold drain from the United States and possibly force a collapse of the international gold exchange standard.[10]

While there is considerable merit in Kindleberger's criticism of the liquidity and official settlements concepts of balance, he has not satisfied those who desire a definitive measure of surplus or deficit for a key currency country. For the critics of the Kindleberger position, the problem hinges on how much liquidity in the form of dollar assets the rest of the world desires to hold, since the rest of the world has alternative assets in which to hold liquidity, including gold. This problem will be considered further in the next two chapters.

Balance of Payments Adjustment

Whatever concept of balance we decide to employ for measuring a payments deficit or surplus, the balance of payments is rarely

[9] Emile Despres, C. P. Kindleberger, and W. S. Salant, "The Dollar and World Liquidity: A Minority View," *The (London) Economist,* February 5, 1966, pp. 526–529.

[10] For a criticism of the Kindleberger position, see George N. Halm, *International Financial Intermediation: Deficits Benign and Malignant,* Essays in International Finance No. 68 (Princeton, N.J.: International Finance Section, Princeton University, June 1968).

in equilibrium, and then only for a fleeting moment, as it moves from deficit to surplus or vice versa. For modern nations with monetary and fiscal and other economic policies directed mainly toward the achievement of such domestic goals as growth and full employment, there are no automatic forces tending to move the balance of payments back to equilibrium as it departs from that point in one direction or another. Concern over the balance of payments may, of course, lead governments to adopt measures which will move the country in the direction of equilibrium, but the adoption of policies for this purpose is nearly always tempered by the priority given to domestic goals.

Deficits (or surpluses), however defined, would not arise if the external value of a country's currency were permitted to move freely with demand and supply forces and without intervention by the government. This does not mean that the adoption of a freely fluctuating exchange rate would do away with balance of payments problems or with the need to consider balance of payments adjustment. An incipient balance of payments deficit would immediately be reflected in a decrease in the exchange value of a country's currency. This usually means a rise in the prices of imports relative to export prices—that is, a decline in the terms of trade.[11] On the other hand, an incipient surplus, which has the effect of raising the foreign exchange value of a country's currency, is not an unmixed blessing since it means that the country's export prices rise relative to prices in other countries while its import prices fall relative to domestic prices and costs. This weakens the competitive position of domestic producers relative to foreign producers. It is also argued that fluctuating exchange rates create risks and uncertainties in trade, and tend to depress international trade. Thus, for a variety of reasons policy makers in most countries have preferred a system of fixed exchange rates, or at least a system of fixed parities above and below which exchange rates move in a narrow range. In order to maintain exchange rates in the face of balance of payments fluctuations, countries use their official foreign exchange reserves or increase their external liabilities in periods

---

[11] A decrease in a country's terms of trade means that the same bundle of export goods buys a smaller bundle of import goods than before.

of balance of payments deficit and increase their reserve holdings (or reduce their liabilities) in periods of balance of payments surplus.

Fluctuations in the balance of payments fall into several categories. First, there are seasonal variations in exports relative to imports. Second, there are fluctuations reflecting cyclical variations in business activity at home and abroad. As a rule, periods of high business activity and full employment tend to raise imports relative to exports, while economic recessions have just the reverse effect. On the other hand, exports of individual countries tend to rise with business expansion abroad and to decline during periods of contraction abroad. Third, there are fluctuations caused by "random factors" such as the Suez crisis in 1956 or the Middle East war of mid-1967, both of which temporarily weakened Britain's balance of payments. Finally, there are longer-term or deep-seated forces making for a persistent surplus or deficit in a country's balance of payments which may continue until some fundamental adjustment occurs, such as a change in monetary and fiscal policies or a devaluation or upward revaluation of the currency.

The first three types of fluctuation are usually dealt with by drawing on reserves or borrowing abroad in the case of deficits or by simply permitting reserves to accumulate in the case of surpluses. The fourth type of situation, if it continues for a long period of time, usually calls for more positive action since for most, if not all, countries large deficits cannot go on indefinitely. The situation is somewhat different in the case of surplus countries; surpluses can continue indefinitely so long as the country is willing to increase its holdings of international reserves. Since governments appear to have an infinitely elastic demand for reserves, corrective action is usually left to the deficit countries.[12]

Exchange Controls

When a country has a persistent balance of payments deficit it may adopt one or a combination of measures including exchange

[12] Except for the amount of new reserves injected into the international payments system, deficits and surpluses of countries (if properly defined) should always be equal for the system as a whole.

controls, monetary and fiscal restraint, or devaluation. Even if a country intends to take more basic adjustment measures, it may seek to halt the drain on its international reserves by means of exchange controls until other measures take effect. Exchange controls may take the form of restrictions on capital exports or controls over payments for imports of goods and services. One type of exchange control involves the use of multiple exchange rates: the foreign exchange required to pay for certain imports is made more expensive than that needed to purchase other, perhaps more essential, imports. At the same time, certain exports, especially those for which both domestic supply and foreign demand are believed to be elastic, may be encouraged by establishing a differential export rate favoring exporters of these commodities.

Controls on capital exports have been employed by many countries for long periods of time and in most cases do not involve a serious distortion in the economy unless they discourage foreign investment in the country. Efforts to prevent residents of a country from exporting capital are easily evaded, however, and many Latin American countries have given up trying to control capital exports in favor of establishing a free exchange market for capital transactions.[13]

Controls over imports of goods and services tend to create domestic price distortions and frequently lead to a misallocation of resources. They enable a country to maintain an overvalued exchange rate which tends to have an adverse effect on exports and works against a fundamental adjustment of the balance of payments.[14]

The Mechanism of Balance of Payments Adjustment: Monetary and Fiscal Restraint vs. Devaluation

It should be emphasized that neither exchange controls nor balance of payments loans from the IMF or other sources constitute an adjustment of the balance of payments when there is a

[13] See Margaret G. deVries, "Multiple Exchange Rates: Expectations and Experiences," IMF *Staff Papers*, July 1965, pp. 282–311.

[14] For a review of exchange control devices see Raymond F. Mikesell, *Foreign Exchange in the Postwar World* (New York: Twentieth Century Fund, 1954).

condition of persistent disequilibrium. In analyzing the adjust-ment process, we shall concentrate on the current account, since for most countries which find themselves in balance of payments deficit the improvement of the current account is the most funda-mental aspect of adjustment. In aggregate terms, a deficit in the current account means that a country is spending more on con-sumption, domestic investment, and government goods and ser-vices than it is producing, the difference being made up with imported resources. Thus, we may write

$$B = Y - E,$$

where B is the current account balance, Y is domestic output, and E is total expenditures (all in real terms). If B is to be increased, domestic expenditures must decline relative to domestic output or domestic output must rise relative to expenditures. We must judge the effectiveness of measures to improve the current account balance on the basis of how they affect these aggregate measures. For example, monetary and fiscal restraints are designed to reduce domestic expenditures; and certainly for countries experiencing inflation coupled with balance of payments deficits, monetary and fiscal restraint will be an effective and necessary means of reducing the deficit. On the other hand, domestic financial restraint may reduce output and thus interfere with an important domestic policy goal.

The basic problem in dealing with a current account deficit, therefore, is to reduce or restrain E (total expenditures) while maintaining or increasing Y (domestic output). This is where a change in the exchange rate may prove effective when coupled with appropriate monetary and fiscal policies. A devaluation of the currency tends to raise the domestic prices of internationally traded goods, both exports and imports, relative to the prices of domestic goods. Thus, devaluation tends to shift domestic expendi-tures away from both imports and those goods which the country may be able to export, while at the same time stimulating exports by increasing the profitability of directing investment to the export industries and output to the export market. In this way it is pos-sible to reduce E relative to Y without reducing Y absolutely, since the reduction in the domestic demand for Y will be compensated by an increase in the foreign demand for Y, while at the same time the decrease in E will reduce imports. This switching of the pattern of both output and expenditure, without an adverse effect on domestic output, calls for a combination of changing the exchange rate and restraining domestic demand.[15] The adjustment may prove to be a delicate and difficult one, especially in economies which tend to be relatively inflexible—that is, where demand and output are not sensitive to changes in relative prices or where there is strong inflation.

If devaluation is employed alone without the accompaniment of appropriate monetary and fiscal policies designed to reduce E relative to Y, any improvement in the current account balance will be short-lived; devaluation alone will reinforce inflationary pressures tending to raise E relative to Y. Only in cases where there is a large amount of unemployed resources, including excess plant capacity, and where there is a high degree of flexibility in the economy, will it be possible by means of a devaluation to raise Y relative to E without fiscal and monetary restraint. This was true in the case of a number of developed countries in the 1930's, but it is generally not true today.

U. S. Balance of Payments Deficits, 1950–1967

As the world's dominant key currency country, the U.S. balance of payments has a major impact upon the international payments system and undoubtedly has a greater impact upon the economies of other countries than it has on the U.S. economy. The changes in the U.S. balance of payments position during the post-World War II period have been dramatic. Immediately following the war until 1950, the United States had a balance of payments surplus

[15] For an excellent discussion of balance of payments adjustment along the lines suggested here, see Harry G. Johnson, "Towards a General Theory of the Balance of Payments," in Richard E. Caves and Harry G. Johnson, eds., *Readings in International Economics* (Homewood, Ill.: Richard D. Irwin, 1968), pp. 374–388.

on the liquidity basis. Foreign countries recovering from the war required time to rebuild their export industries, and all countries were in great need of the products available in abundance only in the United States. A portion of the excess demand for U.S. exports over U.S. imports was financed by U.S. economic and military aid programs. But a considerable portion was financed by the drawing down of foreign countries' gold and dollar reserves. Then in 1950, the U.S. balance of payments on a liquidity basis shifted from a surplus to a deficit position; thereafter, except for virtual balance in 1951 and a small surplus in 1957, it has been in deficit.[16] (See Table 3.)

There were several reasons for the shift in the U.S. liquidity balance beginning in 1950. First, there was a large increase in U.S. imports as a consequence of the Korean war. Second, there was the devaluation of sterling and other European currencies in 1949, which tended to reduce the competitive position of U.S. exports in relation to those of Western Europe. And third, there were large overseas military expenditures occasioned by the Korean war and the building of NATO forces in Europe. It should be noted that U.S. foreign aid (excluding military grants) declined sharply after 1949.

Although the United States continued to have a substantial current account surplus in most years after 1950 (but much lower than the surpluses during the immediate postwar period), private and governmental capital outflow plus government grants exceeded the current account surplus. (See Table 3.) Thus, foreign countries were receiving more dollars than were required to finance the differences between their imports from the United States and what they earned through exports to the United States. U.S. military expenditures overseas rose rapidly during and after the Korean war, reaching a high of $3.4 billion in 1958; then, after declining somewhat, they rose again with the Vietnam conflict to $4.3 billion in 1967. These expenditures, which are included as a part of the current account, have tended to hold down the current account surplus. Nevertheless, the current account surplus rose from $1.8 billion in 1950 to $5.7 billion in 1957 and, after a sharp

[16] Data for calculating the U.S. balance of payments position on the official settlements basis have been available only for the years beginning with 1960.

TABLE 3

U.S. International Transactions, Selected Balances, 1946–1967

(In millions of dollars)

	1946	1947	1948	1949	1950	1951	1952	1953	1954	1955	1956
Merchandise trade balance	6,634	10,036	5,630	5,270	1,009	2,921	2,481	1,291	2,445	2,753	4,575
Current account balance	7,744	11,529	6,440	6,149	1,779	3,671	2,226	386	1,828	2,009	3,967
Balance on liquidity basis	993	4,210	817	136	−3,489	−8	−1,206	−2,184	−1,541	−1,242	−973
Balance on official settlements basis	n.a.	n.a.	n.a.	n.a.	n.a.	n.a.	n.a.	n.a.	n.a.	n.a.	n.a.

	1957	1958	1959	1960	1961	1962	1963	1964	1965	1966	1967[p]
Merchandise trade balance	6,099	3,312	985	4,757	5,444	4,417	5,079	6,676	4,772	3,658	3,483
Current account balance	5,729	2,206	147	4,001	5,509	5,045	5,853	8,462	6,944	5,102	4,798
Balance on liquidity basis	578	−3,365	−3,870	−3,901	−2,370	−2,203	−2,671	−2,800	−1,335	−1,357	−3,575
Balance on official settlements basis	n.a.	n.a.	n.a.	−3,403	−1,347	−2,705	−2,044	−1,549	−1,304	225	−3,398

[p]Preliminary
SOURCE: Walther Lederer and Evelyn M. Parrish, "The Balance of Payments in the First Quarter of 1967," *Survey of Current Business,* June 1967, pp. 22–23, 28–29; and *Survey of Current Business,* March 1968, pp. 23, 25.

decline, rose fairly steadily to a high of $8.5 billion in 1964, a year during which the U.S. deficit on the liquidity basis was $2.8 billion and on the official settlements basis was $1.5 billion. (See Table 3.)

The existence of a U.S. deficit in 1964 in the face of the highest current account surplus since 1947 may be attributed in part to the large U.S. private capital outflow which reached a net total of over $6.5 billion in that year. In addition to net direct investment outflow of $2.4 billion, Americans purchased over a billion dollars in newly issued foreign securities, and U.S. banks and other financial institutions made loans to foreigners totaling (net) some $2.5 billion. Liquid liabilities to foreigners rose by $2.6 billion, of which $1.8 billion represented increased private holdings; the gold loss of $125 million mainly reflected an excess of domestic gold consumption over production rather than net gold sales abroad. While U.S. officials expressed great alarm over the U.S. balance of payments deficit in 1964, this country was performing its world banker function in a rather magnificent manner, both by supplying capital to the rest of the world and by providing an expansion of international liquidity in the form of private and official foreign dollar holdings.

The 1950–1957 Period

Over the period 1950–1957 the United States had a cumulative payments deficit on the liquidity basis of $11.1 billion, but the U.S. Treasury gold stock declined by only $1.7 billion (from $24.6 billion at the end of 1949 to $22.9 billion at the end of 1957). No one was very concerned about the U.S. deficit during the 1950–1957 period. It averaged less than $1.4 billion per year, and there was only a modest decline in the U.S. gold reserves, representing a desirable reversal from the early postwar period; this gold helped to reconstitute the reserves of other countries which had been depleted during the 1940's. The accumulation of U.S. dollar assets by foreigners also served to increase the world supply of international liquidity and provided a desirable supplement to the world monetary reserves, especially since the world's stock of monetary gold was not rising in relation to the increase in world trade.

The Gold Drain After 1957

By contrast, during the period 1958–1967 the cumulative U.S. deficit amounted to $27.4 billion, of which $10.8 billion took the form of a reduction in the gold stock, so that by the end of 1967 U.S. gold holdings were less than half of the 1949 level. The U.S. gold loss during the 1960–1967 period was roughly equal to the amount of gold acquired by the monetary authorities in Europe (Table 4). During the three-year period 1958–1960, the United States had, on the liquidity basis, a cumulative deficit of $11.1 billion, larger than that for the eight-year period 1950–1957, and nearly half of this amount, $5 billion, took the form of gold outflow. During this period, serious concern was expressed regarding the U.S. balance of payments, both in the United States and abroad, but no special actions were taken other than the manipulation of interest rates in a manner designed to limit short-term U.S. capital exports. During the period 1961–1966, a period of relatively rapid economic growth and high levels of employment in the United States, the cumulative U.S. deficit totaled $12.7 billion, or an annual rate of $2.1 billion, as compared with an annual rate of $3.7 billion during the 1958–1960 period, and the gold loss for the 1961–1966 period amounted to $4.6 billion. (See Table 5.)

The reduction in the annual U.S. balance of payments deficit during the 1961–1966 period was largely a consequence of the remarkable improvement in the U.S. surplus on current account, which held the deficit to a modest level in spite of the large increase in private capital outflow. Had it not been for the fairly sizeable gold loss during this period, on top of the $5-billion gold loss during the 1958–1960 period, the balance of payments deficit would probably not have occasioned great concern. From the standpoint of the world economy the increase in foreign dollar holdings of some $2 billion per year provided a desirable supplement to international liquidity. But the continued erosion of U.S. gold reserves indicated a growing preference on the part of foreign central bankers for holding gold rather than dollars, and, in addition, private purchases of gold, both for hoarding and for industrial uses, were expanding.

TABLE 4

International Monetary Reserves, 1960 and September, 1967

(In millions of dollars; end of period)

	Gold		Foreign Exchange		Reserve Position in IMF		Total	
	1960	1967 (Sept.)	1960	1967 (Sept.)	1960	1967 (Sept.)	1960	1967 (Sept.)
World	38,030	40,610	18,665	25,700	3,570	5,894	60,270	72,205
Industrial Countries	33,965	35,385	9,925	13,665	3,218	5,091	47,105	54,135
United States	17,804	13,077	—	1,200	1,555	372	19,359	14,649
United Kingdom	2,801	1,831	430	902	488	—	3,719	2,733
EEC	9,436	15,164	5,704	6,472	785	3,602	15,924	25,235
Other industrial countries	3,926	5,310	3,789	5,087	392	1,118	8,109	11,519
Other developed areas	1,410	2,595	2,260	2,995	135	304	3,800	5,890
Less developed areas	2,660	2,630	6,485	9,045	217	498	9,360	12,175

SOURCE: *International Financial Statistics*, March 1968.

TABLE 5

U.S. Gold Stock, Holdings of Convertible Foreign Currencies, and Reserve Position in IMF, 1958–1968

(In millions of dollars; end of period)

	Total reserve assets	Gold stock[1]		Convertible foreign currencies	Reserve position in IMF
		Total[2]	Treasury		
1958	22,540	20,582	20,534	—	1,958
1959	21,504	19,507	19,456	—	1,997
1960	19,359	17,804	17,767	—	1,555
1961	18,753	16,947	16,889	116	1,690
1962	17,220	16,057	15,978	99	1,064
1963	16,843	15,596	15,513	212	1,035
1964	16,672	15,471	15,388	432	769
1965	15,450	13,806	13,733	781	863
1966	14,882	13,235	13,159	1,321	326
1967—June	14,274	13,169	13,110	738	367
Dec.	14,830	12,065	11,982	2,345	420
1968—March	13,926	10,703	10,484	2,746	477

[1]Includes (a) gold sold to the United States by the International Monetary Fund with the right of repurchase, and (b) gold deposited by the IMF to mitigate the impact on the U. S. gold stock of foreign purchases for the purpose of making gold subscriptions to the IMF under quota increases.
[2]Includes gold in Exchange Stabilization Fund.
SOURCE: *Federal Reserve Bulletin*, April 1968, p. A-68.

Direct Action to Control the U.S. Balance

The U.S. government first took direct action in 1963 to control the balance of payments by means of the Interest Equalization Tax (IET), which is a tax on bonds and stocks purchased by Americans from foreigners in the developed countries—with certain exemptions provided for purchases of new issues of Canada and Japan. This was followed in 1965 by the institution of the "voluntary" restraint programs on loans to foreign countries by U.S. banks and nonbank financial institutions, and by a program of "voluntary" limitation on direct investments by American firms in developed countries. These voluntary programs were altered and tightened from time to time. In January 1968, the program for limiting direct investments was made compulsory, and severe limitations were placed both on new investment and on the reinvestment of profits by American firms in foreign countries.[17]

British Devaluation and the Gold Crisis, 1967–1968

In the fourth quarter of 1967, there was a sharp increase in the U.S. balance of payments deficit when the seasonally adjusted deficit rose to an annual rate of $7.4 billion, and the deficit for the year amounted to $3.6 billion on the liquidity basis and $3.4 billion on the official settlements basis. This deficit was accompanied by a loss of about $1.2 billion in gold. A number of factors contributed to the nearly threefold rise in the liquidity deficit over 1966; these included (1) a deterioration in the merchandise balance occasioned by the sharp rise in imports; (2) an increase of over $600 million in military expenditures abroad, largely as a consequence of the Vietnam war; (3) a significant rise in U.S. foreign travel, accounted for in considerable measure by the Montreal Exposition; (4) a substantial increase in net private lending and purchases of newly issued foreign securities; and (5) the liquidation by the British government of a large block of long-term securities held in the United States. The large gold drain was mainly a consequence of the massive increase in the private demand for gold set off by the British devaluation of November 18, 1967. The United States and other members of the London gold pool[18] sold an estimated $3.5 billion in gold during late 1967 and early 1968. For reasons to be discussed in Chapter 5, these sales were suspended by an agreement of the gold pool members on March 17, 1968.[19] The growing U.S. budget deficit during 1967, together with the sterling devaluation, reduced world confidence in the dollar, or at least reduced the willingness to hold dollars rather than gold. In addition to the measures for the control of capital exports noted above, the

[17] For details of all these programs see U.S. Treasury Department, *Maintaining the Strength of the United States Dollar in a Strong Free World Economy* (Washington, D.C.: U.S. Treasury Department, January 1968).

[18] The London gold pool was established by the United States and certain European nations to maintain the price of gold in the London private market at approximately $35 an ounce.

[19] *Monthly Economic Letter* (New York: First National City Bank of New York, April 1968), p. 40.

Johnson Administration proposed a tax on foreign travel, and there were hints of special taxes on U.S. imports. These developments not only threatened the continuation of the gold exchange standard but also threatened to reverse the movement toward freer world trade and payments which had begun in the 1950's.

How Important to Americans Is the Balance of Payments?

Government officials and private bankers are inclined to make dramatic statements about a grave threat to the dollar arising from U.S. balance of payments deficits without bothering to explain what, specifically, the dollar is threatened with or what the consequences of this undefined calamity would be if it should come to pass. If pressed for details they retreat further into obscurantism by predicting "the complete collapse of the international monetary system" if the United States does not achieve balance of payments equilibrium. Such statements do not promote informed decisions on important policy issues, and many private and public financial officials and specialists are probably not being candid or are substituting clichés for serious thought. In the following paragraphs, we shall try to present the real basis for concern about the U.S. balance of payments deficit.

To begin with, the cost in terms of national welfare of any reduction in the international value of the dollar that might arise from U.S. economic policies will be minor compared to the cost of the deterioration of the dollar's internal value. Commercial imports of goods and services, including foreign travel, represented about 4 percent of U.S. GNP in 1967. If the dollar were to depreciate by 10 percent in terms of all foreign currencies, U.S. residents might have to pay some $3 or $4 billion more for the goods and services they buy from abroad. This loss would be minor compared with the loss of welfare on the part of fixed income receivers and the reduction in allocative efficiency which would accompany a 10 percent rise in the domestic price level during a given year.

A continuation of the U.S. deficit at the 1967 level of $3 or $4 billion annually may not necessarily result in a change in the value of the dollar in terms of foreign currencies. If foreigners prefer to hold gold rather than dollars, the United States might be forced to stop converting dollars into gold at $35 an ounce. It might convert dollar holdings of foreign governments into gold at a higher gold price or it might cease converting dollars into gold at any price. Whether the dollar is devalued in the sense that its exchange value declines in terms of some or all foreign currencies depends upon what happens in the foreign exchange markets. Assuming that in time the United States will lack the foreign currencies (or the means of obtaining them by selling gold or by borrowing from the IMF or other countries) to support the price of the dollar in the foreign exchange markets, the price will decline until demand and supply are equated.

Two important considerations must be kept in mind in analyzing the possibility of a depreciation of the dollar in terms of other currencies. First, if holders of dollars do not have the option of obtaining gold at $35 an ounce, they must decide whether they want to buy gold in the private market at a higher price to increase their holdings of other currencies, such as sterling or Deutsche marks, or continue to hold dollars. The special attraction of holding dollars over other currencies, which characterized the dollar as a world currency, will remain. Since the supply of gold is limited, an increased preference for gold would simply drive up its dollar price but would not necessarily affect the foreign exchange value of the dollar. Will other currencies become relatively more attractive? How many of the foreign holders of liquid dollar assets (totaling about $32 billion) would prefer to hold other currencies instead? Much would depend upon the relative stability of the purchasing power of the dollar, the attractiveness of U.S. capital assets, and the general economic and political stability of the United States, including the (remote) danger of restrictions on the right of foreigners to sell their dollar assets for other currencies. These factors would need to be weighed against the alternative of holding currencies other than the dollar.

The second consideration is that a depreciation of the dollar in terms of any other currency means an appreciation of the value of that currency vis-à-vis the dollar. When one country's currency appreciates in relation to other currencies, the prices of its goods and services rise relative to those of other countries. Which countries are willing to appreciate their currencies, not just against the dollar but against the currencies of all other countries that for one reason or another would not permit their currencies to appreciate vis-à-vis the dollar? Many, if not most, students of international finance believe few countries are prepared to see their currencies appreciate, either because they fear an adverse impact on their balance of payments or because they desire to maintain the competitiveness of their exports in world markets.

It has been suggested that if foreign countries were faced with the alternatives of accumulating dollars or letting their currencies depreciate vis-à-vis the dollar, they would seek to avoid the consequences of either course by raising import duties and establishing export subsidies while allowing their currencies to appreciate in relation to the dollar. In other words, they would offset formal appreciation with *de facto* depreciation. Such measures would, of course, violate the obligations of the General Agreement on Tariffs and Trade (GATT). Alternatively, it is suggested that foreign countries might maintain one price for the dollar in terms of their own currency for trade purposes and another in their capital markets. While the success of such schemes appears doubtful, there is the danger of widespread violations of the international agreements governing trade and exchange practices.

The most serious consequences for world trade and capital movements of continued *large* U.S. balance of payments deficits might be the growth of trade and payments restrictions and a general breakdown of the present system of international economic cooperation, including agreements on tariffs, trade, and foreign exchange practices. Such a development would be harmful to the United States, but it would be more harmful to those countries that are more dependent on trade and upon the smooth functioning of an international capital market. The United States has an economic stake in international monetary order and a responsibility as a leader in the world community to help maintain and strengthen monetary order. Dollar deficits in excess of the amount of dollars the world would be willing to absorb are certainly not in the interest of an orderly and cooperative international monetary system. It should be emphasized, however, that this does not mean the elimination of all dollar deficits. On the contrary, a certain level of dollar deficits is consistent with the proper function of the United States as a world banker.

This question will be considered further in Chapter 5 in the light of the changes that have occurred in the international monetary system during 1968. Meanwhile, we shall discuss the shortcomings of the present system which have provided the basis for proposals for its reform.

3

Shortcomings of the Contemporary International Monetary System

The Bretton Woods System

The Par Values

ALTHOUGH THE ROOTS of the contemporary international monetary system go back at least to the beginning of the 19th century, the ground rules were for the first time formally specified in the Articles of Agreement of the IMF adopted at the United Nations Monetary and Financial Conference at Bretton Woods, New Hampshire, in July 1944. The system adopted was essentially the gold exchange standard,[1] but certain principles were agreed upon which were believed to be an improvement over the way the system operated or failed to operate during the interwar period.

The Bretton Woods system represented something of a compromise between the pre-World War I gold standard and the system of managed currencies which developed after World War I whereby foreign exchange stability was subordinated to domestic policy goals of stability and full employment. Exchange values of

[1] The term "gold exchange standard" began to be widely used following World War I when only a few countries maintained convertibility of their currencies directly into gold at a fixed price; the other "convertible" currencies maintained convertibility into the currencies that were directly convertible into gold. Since World War II, only the United States has maintained direct convertibility into gold, but only for dollars held by foreign monetary authorities.

currencies were to be stabilized within a narrow range of their established parities, but the parities themselves could be changed when a country experienced a condition of "fundamental disequilibrium." Although fundamental disequilibrium was not defined in the IMF Agreement, it has come to mean a condition of persistent disequilibrium not amenable to monetary, fiscal, and other economic measures, except at the cost of significant unemployment or retarded growth. While members must consult the IMF (and in some cases obtain its permission) before changing their exchange parities, and must represent that such change is needed to correct a fundamental disequilibrium, it was not intended that par values would be fixed for all time. The system has been described as "the adjustable peg" in which par value changes were to be made in discreet steps when warranted by balance of payments conditions, but rates were not permitted to fluctuate freely beyond 1 percent on either side of parity (except by special permission of the IMF and for temporary periods). Exchange rates were to be maintained by drawing on or adding to reserves as required. If a country was deemed not to be in fundamental disequilibrium but needed to supplement its reserves in order to finance a temporary and reversible deficit which threatened the exchange value of its currency, it could draw upon the resources of the Fund by buying the required exchange with its own currency. The Fund's resources are derived from gold and national currency subscriptions, the gold portion normally constituting 25 percent of each member's quota subscription.

Exchange Controls and Currency Convertibility

Except during the postwar transition period and in special circumstances with the express permission of the Fund, members have agreed not to maintain the external value of their currencies or to maintain external balance by means of exchange controls on current transactions. Nevertheless, most members of the Fund employ restrictions on current transactions. Moreover, since direct import controls can be exercised by restrictions on trade—restrictions which are not within the jurisdiction of the Fund—countries are free to employ controls on current transactions in the form of import quotas, import licensing, limitations on tourist expenditures of residents, etc., as a means of controlling their balance of payments. But since virtually all members of the IMF are also members of the GATT, they are subject to GATT rules on the use of trade controls. Nevertheless, GATT rules permit many exceptions from the general rule that quantitative restrictions are not to be applied on current trade. The term "convertible currency," as applied to members of the Fund, has therefore come to have a special meaning. A currency is "convertible" if no restrictions are placed on the sale of balances of that currency acquired in the course of current account transactions by nonresidents. In other words, "convertibility" of a currency merely implies unrestricted transferability between nonresidents or from a nonresident to a resident when the currency is acquired as payment in a current account transaction. It does not mean that residents are free to sell their currency to nonresidents for foreign currencies or to convert it into other currencies for whatever purpose they may desire.

The Fund Agreement permitted members to establish controls on international capital movements and, in fact, it required countries obtaining balance of payments assistance from the Fund to control capital exports by its own residents. Hence, there was little in the Fund Agreement which encouraged the establishment of a system of free international capital movements, and there seemed to be little recognition of the importance of such a system —at least among the major developed countries—for the efficient allocation of the world's resources.

The Bretton Woods system was never fully applied to all of its members and, indeed, convertibility (as defined above) of the major currencies of the system was not instituted until 1959, when the discriminatory arrangements maintained under the European Payments Union were terminated. Most of the developing-country members of the Fund continue to have exchange controls, including multiple exchange rates. The IMF has encouraged developing countries to simplify their multiple exchange rate systems, but the use of multiple exchange rates is still widespread, especially in Latin America. Many Latin American countries also employ fluctuating exchange rates and have not established fixed parities with the Fund. Most of the members of the IMF still employ some form of restrictions on current transactions, and it makes little difference in practice whether they are called exchange restrictions or import restrictions. Nevertheless, the vast bulk of the current trade of the developed countries at least is free of quantitative import and exchange restrictions, and the par value system has been observed by the major trading nations. Indeed, one of the criticisms of the adjustable peg system is that most countries have been extremely reluctant to change their par values in the face of continued balance of payments disequilibrium, often resorting to controls or continuous borrowing in order to avoid a change in their par value.

Balance of Payments Assistance

IMF members experiencing balance of payments deficits may draw foreign currencies from the Fund which can be used to support the value of their currency in the foreign exchange market.[2] Drawings are of two types: (1) the *gold tranche,* which is normally equal to 25 percent of a country's quota; and (2) the *credit tranche,* or drawings beyond the amount of the member's gold subscription.[3] Drawings in the amount of the gold tranche have been made available automatically to members. This amount has come to be

[2] In making a drawing, an IMF member "buys" foreign currencies from the Fund with its own currency. The Fund's holdings of a member's currency determine the normal limits of that member's use of Fund resources. Ordinarily a member may not acquire foreign currencies from the Fund beyond the point at which the Fund's holdings of that country's currency exceed 200 percent of its quota. This means, in effect, that the foreign exchange credits available from the Fund are equal to 100 percent of a member's quota. The initial subscription to the Fund will normally be 25 percent of a member's quota payable in gold, plus 75 percent in the national currency of the member. When the member has purchased with its own currency an amount equal to its gold subscription, and in addition has purchased an amount of foreign exchange equal to 100 percent of its quota (the country's normal credit facility), the Fund will then hold, in currency, 200 percent of the country's quota.

[3] Originally gold subscriptions were set at 25 percent of a member's quota or 10 percent of a member's net official holdings of gold and dollars as of September 1946, whichever is lower. For quota increases, 25 percent of the increase in subscription must be paid in gold.

called a member's "reserve position in the Fund" and is counted as a part of its official reserves. The credit tranche drawings are subject to approval by the Executive Directors of the IMF. In the case of credit tranche drawings beyond 25 percent of the quota, the IMF has generally stipulated conditions, such as an agreement on the part of the country to reduce its fiscal deficit or to curtail central bank credit. Sometimes the IMF agrees to permit credit tranche drawings by a member up to a certain amount for a given period of time. These are called "standby credits" and the agreements between a member and the IMF are called "standby agreements."

When members draw foreign currencies from the Fund they agree to repay (repurchase the Fund's holdings of their own currency with gold or convertible currency) by an amount equal to half of any increase in the member's official reserves. Members are in any case required to repay credit drawings within three to five years. Credit tranche drawings (but not gold tranche or automatic drawings) are subject to interest charges which increase with the amount of the drawings as a proportion of the quota and with the length of time before they are repaid.

As of January 1968, quotas of the 107 members of the IMF totaled nearly $21 billion. From 1947, when the Fund began operations, through January 1968, members had drawn $13.8 billion (including gold tranche drawings) and had repaid (repurchased) nearly $7.5 billion. By January 1968, net use of credit tranches was $3.4 billion and aggregate reserve positions of members in the Fund totaled $5.8 billion. In addition to a large volume of convertible currency holdings, the Fund held nearly $5 billion in gold.[4] On the basis of past experience, the Fund would appear to have ample assets for meeting normal requests for drawings. However, the reserves of the IMF would be severely strained if a reserve currency country like the United States or Britain should find it necessary to borrow several billion dollars to deal with the sudden conversion of foreign holdings of its currency. In order to meet such contingencies, in 1962 the IMF entered into an agreement with the major industrial countries (the Group of Ten), under

[4] Current data on IMF drawings and assets may be found in *International Financial Statistics*, published monthly by the International Monetary Fund.

which these countries undertook to lend up to $6 billion to the Fund to enable it to provide massive amounts of assistance to one of their number. This facility is called the General Arrangements to Borrow (GAB) and has been used for making large emergency loans to Britain.

The Major Problems

The present international monetary system has given rise to three major problems which have become the basis for proposals for reform to be discussed in the following chapter: (1) the inadequacy of the volume of international reserves; (2) the vulnerability of the reserve currencies to shifts in the composition of reserve holdings; and (3) the inefficiency of the balance of payments adjustment process. All three problems are interrelated, but we shall take up each in a separate section.

The Volume of International Reserves

Official international monetary reserves, as defined by the International Monetary Fund (and as regarded by most countries), include official holdings of gold, convertible foreign currencies (in the form of foreign bank deposits, treasury bills and other short-term assets, and foreign long-term government securities), and gold tranche positions in the Fund. Changes in the composition and volume of international monetary reserves for selected years between 1913 and 1967 are shown in Tables 6 and 7.[5] (See also Figure A.) Data for these tables covering different periods are not fully comparable, but similar trends may be observed for the periods in which the data in the two tables overlap. The volume of each monetary reserve category fluctuates from year to year. For example, gold holdings of central banks and governments depend not only on new gold production, but upon how much is delivered to the central banks as against being absorbed in private hoards and for industrial uses. In some years official gold holdings have actually declined as a result of the absorption of gold by the private

[5] It should be noted that "the volume of reserves" is defined in a gross sense—i.e., foreign liabilities of the monetary authorities are not subtracted from reserve asset holdings.

FIGURE A
Composition of World Reserves

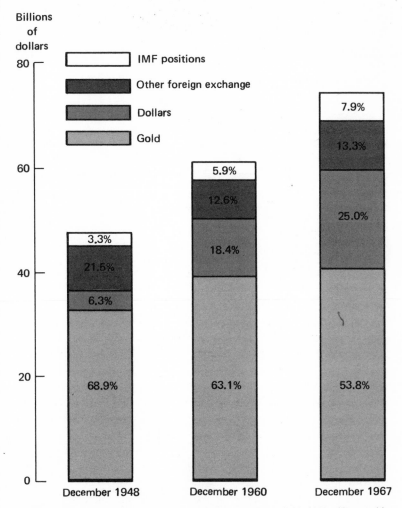

Billions of dollars

IMF positions
Other foreign exchange
Dollars
Gold

80

December 1948
3.3%
21.5%
6.3%
68.9%

December 1960
5.9%
12.6%
18.4%
63.1%

December 1967
7.9%
13.3%
25.0%
53.8%

SOURCE: Board of Governors of the Federal Reserve System, April 30, 1968. (Presented by Secretary of the Treasury Fowler in a statement before the Committee on Foreign Relations, U.S. Senate, May 13, 1968.)

60

TABLE 6

Triffin's Estimates of International Monetary Reserves, Selected Years[a]

(In millions of dollars)

	1913	1922	1933[b]	1933[c]	1949	1957	1962
Gold	4,110	9,850	11,380	19,265	33,500	37,305	39,230
IMF gold tranche	—	—	—	—	1,660	2,315	3,795
Reserve currencies	700	3,160	1,115	1,115	11,710	17,745	22,545
A. U.S. dollars	—	600	60	60	3,200	8,705	12,925
B. Pound sterling	} 700	2,560	1,055	1,055	6,420	6,420	6,220
C. Other currencies and discrepancies					2,090	2,620	3,400
Total	4,810	13,010	12,495	20,385	46,870	57,365	65,570

[a]Official holdings of countries, excludes international institutions.
[b]Gold valued at $20.67 per ounce.
[c]Gold valued at $35 per ounce.
SOURCE: Robert Triffin, *The Evolution of the International Monetary System: Historical Reappraisal and Future Prospectives*, Princeton Studies in International Finance, No. 12 (Princeton, N. J.: International Finance Section, Princeton University, 1964), Table 8, pp. 66–67.

TABLE 7

Estimates of International Monetary Reserves, Selected Years

(In millions of dollars; end of period)

	1948	1949	1958	1959	1965	1966	1967
Gold	33,065	33,470	33,030	37,880	41,850	40,900	39,505
IMF gold tranche	1,560	1,658	2,557	3,250	5,376	6,330	5,748
Foreign exchange	13,365	10,390	17,005	16,220	23,015	24,385	28,330
A. Dollars[a]	—	—	—	10,120	15,372	13,656	15,687
B. Other[b]	—	—	—	6,100	7,643	10,719	12,643
Total	47,990	45,515	57,590	57,355	70,245	71,615	73,583

[a]Liquid dollar liabilities to official institutions in foreign countries.
[b]Residual.
SOURCE: *International Financial Statistics*, various issues; U. S. dollar holdings from *Federal Reserve Bulletin*, July 1968, p. A-74.

61

market in an amount exceeding new world supply.[6] Increases in gold holdings have made virtually no contribution to official reserves since 1965, and in that year such holdings were nearly $2 billion more than they were in 1967, largely as a consequence of the increase in the private demand over new free world supply. Reserve positions in the Fund have increased from time to time as a consequence of the expansion of Fund membership and periodic increases in the quotas of individual members. Since members must subscribe gold to the IMF equal to increases in their reserve positions, increases in IMF quotas do not result in net increases in total reserves. Reserve positions in the Fund may also fluctuate as a result of credit drawings by members since the drawing by one member of the currency of another will improve the position in the Fund of the country whose currency is drawn. Thus, if Britain draws $100 million (in U.S. currency) from the Fund, the U.S. reserve position in the Fund will rise by a corresponding amount.

The volume of reserve currency holdings is subject to substantial fluctuation. The volume may rise when reserve currency countries experience deficits and fall when they have surpluses. Drawings and repayments of reserve currencies from the IMF will also affect reserve currency reserves. When a country reduces its official holdings of a reserve currency, as for example when it buys gold from the U.S. Treasury with its U.S. dollar holdings, there is an automatic reduction in the total volume of international reserves. Thus, during the period 1928–1933, countries drew down their holdings of dollars, sterling, and other reserve currencies so that this category of reserves decreased by about 60 percent. (See Table 6.) There was also a sharp reduction of about $3 billion in reserve currency holdings between 1948 and 1949 as a consequence of the 1949 sterling crisis and devaluation, and this, in turn, led to a reduction in total reserves by about $2.5 billion.[7] (See Table 6.) Official holdings of reserve currencies may fluctuate as a conse-

[6] Additions to free world supplies of gold arise mainly from increases in gold output and gold sales by the USSR. Soviet sales are quite erratic, ranging in recent years from $200 million to $550 million annually. There were virtually no Soviet gold sales during 1967.

[7] The devaluation of sterling in September 1949 lowered the dollar value of sterling reserves. A similar situation occurred in November 1967 when sterling was again devalued.

quence of shifts in foreign exchange holdings between private banks and individuals and the central bank or treasury. Thus, during certain periods U.S. liquid dollar liabilities to foreigners may remain the same, but foreign official holdings of dollars may decline. In such cases, the net reserve position of the United States, as measured by the change in the liquidity balance (change in U.S. official reserve assets minus increase in liquid dollar liabilities to foreigners), may not change, while at the same time foreign official reserve assets may decline.[8] This asymmetrical character of net reserve positions is a consequence of the way in which changes in reserve positions are defined under the liquidity balance concept. This situation is avoided by the official settlements concept of balance.

As Figure A shows, increases in reserve currency holdings during the post-World War II period have made the most important contribution to the increase in the total volume of international reserves. Yet, it is this component that has proved to be the most volatile and vulnerable to decrease under the present international monetary system.

The IMF supplements the reserves of members when they make use of the credit drawing facility. Credit facilities, however, are not the same as reserves because credit drawings must be repaid to the Fund, normally within three to five years. In addition, there is a certain reluctance on the part of governments to finance their deficits by going into debt. Thus, an increase in the volume of credit availabilities will not ordinarily have the same effect on world trade as an equivalent expansion in the volume of world reserves. Since some students of the international monetary system have proposed more liberal credit facilities as against a direct increase in the total volume of reserves, this distinction between reserves and credit facilities is important.

Official reserves by no means constitute the whole of international liquidity. Large amounts of dollars, sterling, and other foreign currency assets are held by foreign banks, firms, and individuals

---

[8] Assume for example that foreign central banks sold $100 million (in U.S. currency) to their own commercial banks. The net reserve position of the United States would remain unchanged and foreign reserve assets would decline by $100 million.

throughout the world. For example, private foreign banks, firms, and individuals held nearly $16 billion in U.S. bank deposits and other short-term dollar assets and marketable government bonds in December 1967.[9] Over $11 billion of these liquid dollar liabilities were held by foreign commercial banks, and about two-thirds of the liquid dollar assets held by foreign commercial banks and non-banking concerns and individuals were demand deposits in U.S. banks. Thus, the bulk of this privately held international liquidity performs the important function of financing world trade and facilitating capital formation throughout the world.

The Composition of Reserves

The viability of the gold exchange standard depends upon the interchangeability of the different kinds of reserve assets at par, and the avoidance of massive flights from one reserve asset to another. The link between reserve currencies and gold has been the willingness of the U.S. Treasury to sell gold at $35 per ounce, for dollars held by foreign monetary authorities, plus the obligation of all IMF members to purchase gold at par against their own currencies when offered by the IMF. Between 1961 and March 1968, there was also a link between reserve currencies and the private gold markets through the action of the members of the London gold pool in maintaining the free market price of gold close to $35 per ounce. The operations of the London gold pool avoided a two-price system for gold but resulted in a drain of official gold into the private market, a drain which assumed very large proportions following the sterling devaluation of November 18, 1967. On the other hand, a two-price system for gold could itself tend to drain gold away from the reserves of the United States by encouraging governments to sell gold for dollars at the free market price and to replenish their gold holdings at the official price from the U.S. Treasury, unless there was a firm agreement to the contrary. Such an agreement was reached by the members of the London gold pool on March 17, 1968, when they decided to discontinue holding down the private market price for gold and agreed not to sell gold

[9] *Federal Reserve Bulletin*, March 1968, p. A–70; see also "Foreign Liquid Assets in the United States," *Monthly Review* (New York: Federal Reserve Bank of New York, June 1968), pp. 117–125.

to monetary authorities to replace gold sold in private markets.[10] Thus, the United States will not knowingly sell gold to governments that have sold gold in the private markets, nor will it buy gold directly or indirectly from private sources.

The gold exchange standard places a special burden on key currency countries in maintaining, directly or indirectly, the parity of their currencies with gold. Except by special agreement, there is no obligation on the part of governments to maintain any particular ratio between gold and reserve currencies. The key currency countries may be compelled to raise interest rates in order to induce foreigners not to withdraw funds by shifting them to other countries, or, in the case of the United States, by presenting the dollars for conversion into gold.[11] If the United States, as the dominant key currency country, avoids a deficit in its balance of payments by restraining domestic credit to a greater degree than is desirable from the standpoint of domestic price stability, it is doing a disservice to its own economy and perhaps to the world economy as well since, in the absence of other sources of world liquidity, dollar deficits may be required in order to expand the volume of international liquidity as world trade and financial transactions grow. This is not to say that a reserve currency country should not employ domestic policies designed to maintain reasonable price stability. It has an obligation to maintain confidence in its currency at home and abroad, but this is not the same as maintaining confidence in its ability to withstand any amount of flight from its currency into gold. Yet, this is a problem inherent in the present international monetary system.

The holders of reserve currencies may also be faced with a problem. There is always a risk in holding a reserve currency as against gold because reserve currencies may be devalued in relation to gold and to other currencies. In the case of the pound sterling this has happened twice since World War II.

Gold is the primary reserve asset under the present monetary

[10] For the text of the central bankers' communiqué see Appendix B.

[11] See Herbert G. Grubel, "The Benefits and Costs of Being the World Banker," *The National Banking Review*, I (December 1964), pp. 189–212. For a contrary view see Henry N. Goldstein, "Does It Necessarily Cost Anything to Be the 'World Banker'?" *The National Banking Review*, II (March 1965), pp. 411–415.

system, and the preference for gold has tended to grow as the ratio of gold to total reserve assets declines. On the other hand, some governments feel that they have an obligation to hold dollars or sterling to prevent the collapse of the present system. This is true of certain members of the sterling area who continue to hold sterling in spite of Britain's weak long-term international financial position; it is also true of certain countries that hold dollars. For these reasons, some students of international finance have proposed the elimination of reserve currencies as reserve assets and their substitution by deposits in the IMF. Others have proposed an increase in the value of gold reserves (to be achieved simply by raising its official price) and the liquidation of foreign exchange holdings by monetary authorities.[12] It is believed that by getting rid of reserve currencies in favor of gold alone, or of gold plus transferable IMF credits, the vulnerability of the system to a flight from reserve currencies into gold, or from one reserve currency into another, such as from sterling into dollars, could be avoided.

It is doubtful, however, that the world can get rid of the reserve currency system simply by an international agreement redefining official reserves. Central banks would still want to hold a portion of their assets in key currencies, both as operating balances and as a means of holding liquidity which earns interest. There would remain a large volume of privately held key currency assets, and at times commercial banks would want to exchange their foreign exchange assets for their own currencies by selling them to their central bank. Certainly, before abolishing reserve currencies it would be well to consider the effects of such an action on the world banker functions of the key currency countries. Many economists hold the view that if gold and reserve currencies are incompatible as alternative means of holding reserves, it would be better to get rid of gold as a reserve medium.

It should also be said that gold could undermine other types of reserve assets, such as deposits in the IMF, under a system in which

[12] If the official price of gold doubled, the U.S. Treasury would have, as of June 1968, $21.4 billion worth of gold instead of $10.7 billion and could redeem the $14.4 billion in liquid dollar obligations to foreign governments. This option would not be open to Britain, however, because of its relatively small gold holdings in relation to its liquid liabilities to foreigners.

gold remains the primary reserve asset. Given a free choice between holding gold or IMF deposits, countries might prefer gold to the extent that there would be a problem of maintaining parity between gold and IMF reserve deposits. As we shall see, this has been an important criticism of the original Triffin plan for international monetary reform.

The Problem of Adjustment

THE RULES OF THE GAME

The traditional textbook explanation of the adjustment process under the gold standard system is based on the assumption that a change in a country's gold and foreign exchange reserves triggers a change in the volume of domestic money in the same direction. Since by the late nineteenth century most countries had central banks which exercised control over domestic money and credit, the relationship between movements in central bank reserves and the volume of domestic money was supposed to have been achieved by the adherence of central banks to "the rules of the game." According to Ragnar Nurkse, adherence to the rules of the game required concurrent changes in the same direction in the international and domestic assets of a central bank.[13] In a study prepared for the League of Nations, Nurkse made a statistical comparison of the annual changes in the international and domestic assets of 26 central banks during the 1922–1938 period and found that in nearly every case these changes were more often in the opposite than in the same direction. Nurkse concluded that the failure of the gold exchange standard during the interwar period was largely a consequence of a failure of central banks to observe the rules of the game, while the success of the gold standard during the pre-World War I period was a consequence of broad adherence to rules of the game.

More recent research has indicated that whatever success was achieved by the international gold standard prior to 1914 was probably not due to the behavior of central banks in accordance with

[13] Ragnar Nurkse, *International Currency Experience* (Geneva: League of Nations, 1944), p. 66.

the rules of the game. Arthur Bloomfield has found that over the 1880–1913 period, year-to-year changes in international and domestic assets of central banks more often were in the opposite direction than in the same direction.[14] This would indicate that central banks tended to expand their own credit to counteract rather than reinforce the effects on the domestic monetary system of international reserve flows. Bloomfield also found that for five of the eleven central banks which he studied, "discount rates and reserve ratios did not characteristically move in opposite directions." This indicated that the link between interest rate changes and movements of gold was not so close or so general under the pre-1914 gold standard as had been supposed.[15] Nevertheless, the one-third of a century before World War I was a period of relative exchange rate stability and liberal trade policies compared with the half century following that war.

Various reasons have been advanced to explain why the gold standard seemed to work so well in the pre-World War I period. These include the parallel movements in prices among the major trading countries, reflecting the operation of competitive forces in relatively open economies; the relatively free movement of international capital and the large capital flows, particularly from Europe to the developing countries of the nineteenth century; and the rise in the volume of reserves and the increase in the efficiency of their use occasioned by a series of fortuitous events, such as the discovery of gold in South Africa and the substitution of paper and deposit money for gold coins.[16] After a period of exchange rate instability following World War I, nations reestablished fixed gold parities during the mid-1920's and attempted to regulate their domestic monetary systems to achieve internal stability. They accomplished neither, and the 1930's saw both a worldwide depression and international monetary chaos.

[14] Arthur I. Bloomfield, *Monetary Policy under the International Gold Standard: 1880–1914* (New York: Federal Reserve Bank of New York, October 1959), pp. 47–51.

[15] *Ibid.*, pp. 31–32.

[16] See Robert Triffin, *The Evolution of the International Monetary System: Historical Reappraisal and Future Prospectives*, Princeton Studies in International Finance No. 12 (Princeton, N.J.: International Finance Section, Princeton University, 1964), pp. 3–20.

ADJUSTMENT UNDER THE BRETTON WOODS SYSTEM

The Bretton Woods system established after World War II was designed to avoid both fluctuating exchange rates and exchange and trade controls on the one hand, and externally induced depressions on the other. It has been only moderately successful in the latter goal and even less successful in the former. The system was supposed to avoid the necessity of balance of payments adjustment at the expense of full employment and growth. This was to be accomplished by the provision of balance of payments assistance for countries having temporary and reversible deficits and by changes in par values in situations where the deficit was of a long-term or chronic nature. The shortcomings of this system have arisen from four principal causes: (a) the reluctance of countries to adjust their currency parities in the face of chronic deficits or surpluses; (b) the failure of some countries to adopt monetary and fiscal policies necessary for sustaining external equilibrium at any exchange rate established for a reasonable period of time; (c) the failure of the system to provide for an adequate growth of international reserves; and (d) the vulnerability of the reserve currency countries to massive withdrawals of reserve currency holdings. Causes (a) and (b) above are concerned specifically with balance of payments adjustments, while (c) and (d) contributed to the failure to create an environment which facilitates adjustment.

Reluctance to Adjust Parities. Contrary to the intention of the authors of the Bretton Woods Agreement, nearly all countries have viewed devaluation as an economic and political disaster and as evidence of the failure of either the government or of the international economic environment. But there is no reason to believe that immutable exchange parities are compatible with monetary and fiscal policies oriented to domestic economic goals in a world of shifting trade structures, differential rates of productivity growth, and differing rates of increase in prices and incomes. The reluctance to change official parities has led governments to impose controls on trade, to use multiple exchange rates and similar devices, and to engage in large short-term borrowing to cover deficits that are neither temporary nor reversible. Both developed and developing countries have been guilty of these practices. It is this attitude toward changing official parities that constitutes the strongest argument for a flexible rate system. The so-called adjustable peg system has failed mainly because it has never been permitted to work according to the intentions of the framers of the Bretton Woods Agreement.

A special problem exists with respect to the alteration of exchange parities by reserve currency countries. The devaluation of a key currency reduces the value of the reserve currency assets of foreign holders in terms of other currencies. Undoubtedly, this was an important factor in the reluctance of Britain to devalue both before September 1949 and before November 1967. In addition, the devaluation of a key currency cannot be an isolated event; it usually involves a readjustment of the currency values of a number of countries. Thus, the 31 percent sterling devaluation of September 1949 was accompanied by a general readjustment of European and sterling area currencies, a fact which greatly reduced the effectiveness of the sterling devaluation. The November 1967 sterling devaluation (14.3 percent) was less drastic (partly because of fear of retaliation by other countries) and led to readjustments by a smaller number of countries, none of which was important in world trade. Any attempt to devalue the dollar would call forth a general readjustment of exchange parities so that a general appreciation of most major currencies vis-à-vis the dollar is probably impossible to achieve. Desirable adjustments in the exchange value of the dollar would be much easier if a few chronic surplus countries were to appreciate their currencies. However, the governments of surplus countries are under strong pressures not to appreciate because of the effects of such action on the competitive position of their exporters and producers of domestic products which compete with imports.[17]

Monetary and Fiscal Policies. As was pointed out in Chapter 2, exchange depreciation alone cannot achieve an improvement in the

[17] Germany appreciated the Deutsche mark by 5 percent in 1961, but the adjustment was not sufficient to avoid that country's large surpluses since 1961. At the time of the French balance of payments crisis in November 1968, pressure was brought upon Germany to appreciate the Deutsche mark but Germany refused in spite of its large surplus.

balance of payments except under favorable conditions. An improvement in the balance must come from a reduction in spending relative to domestic output. Therefore, for countries experiencing inflationary pressures, devaluation without restrictive monetary and fiscal measures sufficient to hold down spending relative to real output will only increase the rate of inflation. Uncontrolled spending together with a completely uncontrolled exchange rate would soon produce hyperinflation (a classic example of which occurred in Germany following World War I) and a complete breakdown of the monetary system. In most countries with so-called flexible rate systems, the rate of external depreciation of the currency has tended to lag behind the rate of internal depreciation.[18] This gives rise to an overvalued exchange rate which tends to hamper exports and the achievement of balanced trade except with the use of trade controls.[19]

Inadequate World Reserves. In discussions of the adjustment process, it is usually assumed that countries with balance of payments deficits will eliminate their deficits at the expense of countries with surpluses. This assumes that the surplus countries are willing to cooperate in the adjustment process by allowing their surpluses to melt away and at times to accept a deficit position as trade and capital movements respond to the measures taken by other countries seeking to restore equilibrium. Under this hypothesis, countries need reserves to tide them over periods of deficits, the magnitude of the required reserves being based on past experience and expectations for the future.

This hypothesis, unfortunately, is not well-founded in the behavioral pattern of central bankers. For some countries the desirable state of affairs is a surplus over time accompanied by a more or less continuous accumulation of reserves. Whenever their positive balance disappears or a deficit occurs they are unwilling to allow their reserves to decline (or even to fail to rise) but rather

[18] A major exception was Canada after that country adopted a flexible exchange rate in 1949.

[19] See Raymond F. Mikesell, *Inflation in Latin America*, Subcommittee on American Republics Affairs, Committee on Foreign Relations, U.S. Senate (Washington, D.C.: USGPO, September 1967), pp. 20–21.

take restrictive actions to restore their former position. Such countries are unwilling to use their reserves for the very purpose for which presumably they were accumulated, mainly to cover their payments deficits without restraining the domestic economy until the pendulum again swings back toward a surplus.[20]

This situation makes difficult the problem of adjustment by countries whose monetary authorities are unwilling to take restrictive action in response to a deficit which they believe to be a consequence of temporary forces. Indeed, unless surplus countries are willing to give up their surpluses and, perhaps, occasionally go into deficit, balance of payments adjustment becomes impossible with a fixed volume of international reserves. But if world reserves are expanding at a sufficient rate, deficit countries can get into balance without eliminating the surpluses of other countries. A U.S. Treasury Department study suggests that increases in the total volume of reserves might cover half of the reserve losses experienced by deficit countries; in other words, only half of the reserve gains would be at the expense of reserve losses of other countries.[21]

The problem of the rate at which total world reserves should be increased is a difficult and controversial one. On the one hand, the higher the rate of increase in reserves, the smaller the number and the amounts of deficits and consequently the smaller the pressures for restrictions on trade and capital movements. On the other hand, it is feared by some that too large a rate of increase in world reserves will contribute to world inflation since countries would be less constrained to limit their expenditures.[22] It is virtually impossible to determine in advance the optimum level of international liquidity, since it is not possible to predict the reactions of governments and central banks to change in their international reserve

[20] See Fritz Machlup, "The Need for Monetary Reserves," Banca Nazionale del Lavoro *Quarterly Review*, Rome, September 1966.

[21] George A. Willis and Fred L. Springborn, *The Need for International Reserves* (Washington, D.C.: U.S. Treasury Department, September 1967), p. 6.

[22] If new reserves are allocated to a country, that country can run a deficit by the amount of the acquisition of new reserves without a loss of reserves. Likewise, it is argued that so long as the United States can create dollar liabilities which other countries are willing to hold, the United States will not restrain its foreign deficits.

positions. Many European central bankers believe that there is already too much international liquidity, and that this tends to promote worldwide inflation. However, inflation is mainly a consequence of internal monetary and fiscal policy, and countries can always take steps to avoid the inflationary impact of a balance of payments surplus by appropriate monetary action. In many cases, surplus countries could also reduce their surpluses by liberalizing their trade and payments. While we cannot determine with any certainty what the optimum rate of increase in international reserves would be in terms of maximizing world welfare, most economists believe that the world would gain from a substantially higher rate of increase in international reserves than we have seen in recent years.

Vulnerability of Reserve Currencies. As has already been noted, the expansion of world reserves in recent years has depended almost entirely upon the growth of liquid dollar assets which, in turn, has been a consequence of U.S. balance of payments deficits. But this has increased the vulnerability of the dollar to increases in the demand for gold since reserve asset holders are convinced that the value of gold will never be depreciated in terms of reserve currencies but that reserve currencies may depreciate in terms of gold.[23]

The present international monetary system provides no clear answers to the problem of adjustment for a reserve currency country. The United States, for reasons indicated earlier, may not have the option of devaluation; it should not employ exchange controls which impair its role as world banker; and its balance of payments is, in part, the result of forces operating in the international financial system and only partly a consequence of its internal policies. The gold exchange standard worked reasonably well in the pre-1914 period when sterling was the sole reserve currency, but the position of sterling as a reserve currency has been weakened during much of the period since World War I, when the reserve currency

---

[23] See Howard S. Piquet, "Some Consequences of Dollar Speculation in Gold," in *Factors Affecting the Balance of Payments of the United States,* U.S. Congress, Joint Economic Committee, 87th Cong., 2nd sess. (Washington, D.C.: USGPO, 1962).

role of sterling had to be shared with the dollar. In order to perform its world banker function properly, a reserve currency country must, over time, run deficits. As has been shown by the experience of the United States, these deficits may be substantial even when there is a large current account surplus. This was the case in 1964 when the U.S. current account surplus was nearly $8.5 billion (excluding military grants), while the deficit under the liquidity concept was $2.8 billion. Yet, the obligation to convert foreign balances into gold constitutes a continual threat to the reserve currency country, a threat which the monetary authorities in the United States have sought to mitigate by capital controls which impair its financial intermediary functions. Moreover, if we admit that inflationary tendencies in the U.S. economy have contributed in part to the deficit, particularly in 1966 and 1967 when the current account surplus declined sharply, there is still a dilemma arising from the fact that neither devaluation nor capital controls constitute proper remedies for a reserve currency country.

4

Proposals for Reforming the International Monetary System

OVER THE PAST DECADE there have been a number of proposals for changing the international monetary system in order to deal with one or more of the problems outlined in the previous chapter. While all of these proposals cannot be neatly categorized, it is convenient for our analysis to divide them as follows:

1. Proposals to improve the operation of the present system without fundamental alteration.
2. Proposals to replace reserve currency holdings with gold.
3. Proposals to replace reserve currency holdings with a new form of international reserve asset.
4. Proposals to supplement existing reserves with a new form of reserve asset.
5. Proposals to demonetize gold.
6. Proposals to change the par value system in favor of flexible exchange rates.

Proposals to Improve the Operation of the Present System

For years economists and bankers have been making recommendations for improving the present international monetary system. Among the recommended improvements are (a) an extension of the gold exchange standard to include more reserve currencies and the greater use of reserve currencies in reserve assets; (b) a higher degree of central bank cooperation, especially in dealing with hot money flows; and (c) larger and more liberal credit facilities through the IMF. Many of the specific proposals to improve the operation of the present international monetary system without fundamentally changing it have already been implemented. Among these proposals have been (a) increasing the quotas of the members of the IMF; (b) expanding liquidity by means of swap arrangements whereby one country agrees to sell its currency against the currency of another country; (c) arrangements for the IMF to supplement its resources by borrowing from the major developed countries; and (d) supplementing official reserve holdings of dollars and sterling with other currencies, thereby broadening the reserve currency base.

The quotas of *all* IMF members were increased by 50 percent in 1959 and by 25 percent in 1966; some quotas were increased even more. These quota increases did not raise the reserves of the members since the increase in automatic drawing rights was offset by the requirement to subscribe 25 percent of the additions to the quotas in gold. Only the normal credit drawing facilities of the members were increased. In addition, the IMF has liberalized the drawing rights of developing countries which experience deficits as a consequence of falling export prices for primary commodities. Thus, under certain circumstances, members may draw an amount of foreign exchange from the IMF equal to 50 percent of their quota (but no more than 25 percent in any twelve-month period), this amount being over and above the normal credit drawing rights (or 100 percent of the quota) of the member.

In 1961, the U.S. monetary authorities began using foreign currencies to support the value of the dollar in the exchange markets rather than relying solely on the convertibility of the dollar into gold. These currencies have been acquired from other countries through swap transactions and the sale of bonds to foreign monetary authorities. As of September 6, 1968, the Federal Reserve System had entered into swap arrangements totaling nearly $10 billion, although only a portion of this amount had actually been drawn. As of December 27, 1967, the United States had acquired

$1.8 billion in foreign currencies under these arrangements, but this amount declined to only $130 million by September, 1968.[1] In addition, the United States, as of September 6, 1968, had sold $2.0 billion (equivalent) of medium-term (Roosa) bonds to foreign central banks in exchange for foreign currencies and dollars.[2] The foreign currencies provide a means of supporting the exchange value of the dollar without the use of gold. The swap transactions also add to both U.S. and world liquidity since foreign holders of dollars under the swaps count the dollars as a part of their official reserves.

In 1962, the Group of Ten[3] concluded an arrangement whereby they would loan their currencies to the IMF in the aggregate equivalent of $6 billion, the idea being that such a currency pool could be used by the Fund, when required, to make credits available to Group members for combating large capital outflows, or to provide confidence when such outflows seem imminent. While the IMF has substantial assets for dealing with temporary balance of payments deficits arising from current account deficits of most of its members, it could not afford to employ several billion dollars of its assets to provide massive aid to a reserve currency country such as Britain or the United States. Advances under the General Arrangements to Borrow (GAB) are included as a part of monetary reserves of the lenders. On several occasions credits made available through the GAB were extended to the United Kingdom for dealing with sterling crises.

The U.S. government has included in its reserve assets foreign convertible currencies in amounts which at times have been well

[1] *Monthly Review* (New York: Federal Reserve Bank of New York, September 1968), pp. 179–180.

[2] *Ibid.*, p. 181.

[3] Members of the Group of Ten include Belgium, Canada, France, Germany, Italy, Japan, the Netherlands, Sweden, the United Kingdom, and the United States. The ministerial representatives of the Group of Ten countries, which include both finance ministers and governors of central banks, meet from time to time to make reports and recommendations to their governments. Important studies have been carried on by the deputies to the ministers and governors. Indeed, the Group of Ten has become the most powerful international financial policy-making body in the world. It was this group that reached agreement on the new reserve asset, Special Drawing Rights (SDRs), which will be discussed later in this chapter.

over $2 billion (equivalent). Included are Belgian francs, Canadian dollars, Deutsche marks, Dutch guilders, Austrian schillings, Swiss francs, and Italian lire, among others. These currencies have been accumulated largely as a consequence of swap transactions and the sale of Roosa bonds, since the continuous U.S. deficit has made it difficult to earn foreign currencies.[4] However, there are important limitations on expanding the number of currencies which might be held as reserves by monetary authorities. These include the lack of short-term investment facilities in most countries, and the fact that balances in one currency are not always fully usable for making payments to a third country. Thus, it is difficult to expand the number of currencies employed as official reserves when the countries lack the basic institutions associated with reserve currency countries.

Central Bank Cooperation

Central bank cooperation has worked well in recent years, notably during the Suez crisis of 1956–1957, the Cuban missiles crisis, and the crisis of confidence accompanying the sterling devaluation of November 1967.[5] It has also eased the impact of U.S. deficits on Treasury gold stocks. The governments of major industrial countries have a large stake in preserving the present monetary system and, in spite of frequent admonitions to the United States and to Britain to reduce their balance of payments deficits, cooperation in dealing with international monetary difficulties has been readily forthcoming. Nevertheless, these arrangements have been in the nature of palliatives rather than cures of the fundamental shortcomings of the gold exchange standard. Credit facilities are not a substitute for reserves at hand, nor do they provide for a permanent expansion in the volume of international liquidity. Thus, many economists have come to believe

[4] For a discussion of the advantages of increased foreign currency holdings, see "Conversations on International Finance," *Monthly Review* (New York: Federal Reserve Bank of New York, August 1963), pp. 114–121; see also "Treasury and Federal Reserve Foreign Exchange Operations," *Monthly Review* (New York: Federal Reserve Bank of New York, March 1968), pp. 38–52.

[5] Large amounts of foreign currency credits, including swap arrangements, were made available to Britain both before and after the sterling devaluation of November 1967.

that, no matter how liberal the credit facilities available for meeting temporary deficits and crises of confidence, such facilities will not provide the kind of environment necessary for balance of payments adjustment and the avoidance of direct controls on trade and payments.

The Group of Ten

Beginning in 1963, the representatives of the Group of Ten countries participating in the GAB began a serious study of the need for supplementing existing reserves and of various proposals for changing the international monetary system. However, the Group's first report on the functioning of the international monetary system, issued in August 1964, indicated no immediate need for a change in the system, although it did suggest that in the longer run some new type of reserve asset might be required.[6] During the following months, the deputies of the Group of Ten studied various proposals and approaches to the creation of additional reserve assets and in 1965 issued an analytical study entitled *Report of the Study Group on the Creation of Reserve Assets*.[7] By mid-1965, the U.S. government, as well as the governments of most of the Group of Ten countries, had reached the conclusion that serious negotiations should be initiated within the Group of Ten and later with the International Monetary Fund on a new plan for reserve creation. These negotiations, which led to the adoption in 1967 of the plan for Special Drawing Rights in the IMF, will be discussed later in this chapter.

Proposals to Replace Reserve Currency Holdings with Gold

The best-known advocate of replacing present reserve currency holdings with gold is the French economist, Jacques Rueff, an economic advisor to President de Gaulle and a former Vice-Gov-

[6] "Ministerial Statement of the Group of Ten and Annex," prepared by the deputies to the Group of Ten, August 10, 1964; for text see the *Federal Reserve Bulletin*, August 1964, pp. 975–999.

[7] This report, which is often referred to as the Ossola Report after the chairman of the study group, was released by the Group of Ten in August 1965.

ernor of the Bank of France.[8] Rueff's views take on special significance as the economic rationale for the French government's current position on the international monetary system—a position
which has been sharply at variance with that of the United States
and most other governments. Rueff calls for the abolition of the
gold exchange standard and a "return" to the automatic gold standard under which all official reserves would be held in gold, deficits
would be settled in gold, and the outflow of gold would be permitted to put pressure on the domestic monetary system sufficient
to reverse balance of payments deficits. There is, according to
Rueff, no present shortage of liquidity, and any future needs for
additional liquidity can be met by increased gold production,
which is spurred by falling commodity prices. The present system
of reserve creation through the balance of payments deficits of the
reserve currency countries, the United States and Britain, makes
impossible the operation of the adjustment mechanism under the
gold standard rules and should be brought to an end by the refusal
of countries to accept dollars and sterling as a part of their official
reserves.

Rueff suggests that the U.S. liabilities to reserve currency
holders be liquidated. A general increase in the price of gold from
$35 to $70 per ounce would raise the dollar value of U.S. gold
holdings sufficiently to enable this country to redeem its outstanding dollar obligations in gold. Since Britain's gold reserves are in-
sufficient to repay holders of sterling balances with the profit from
gold revaluation, Rueff suggests that the countries whose reserves
would be increased in value by gold revaluation make a long-term
loan to Britain to enable it to liquidate sterling obligations held
by monetary authorities.

It is a little difficult to comprehend how a contemporary economist can seriously advocate the automatic gold standard in an age
when all governments are politically committed to giving first

[8] For a statement of Rueff's position see Jacques Rueff, "The Rueff Ap-
proach," in Randall Hinshaw (ed.), *Monetary Reforms and the Price of Gold:
Alternative Approaches* (Baltimore: Johns Hopkins Press, 1967), pp. 37–46.
Somewhat similar views are held by M. A. Heilperin in "The Case for Going
Back to Gold," *Fortune*, September 1962, pp. 108–110, 144–159.

priority to domestic goals. Moreover, Rueff appears to have accepted without question the myth of the pre-1914 gold standard as operating smoothly in accordance with the rules of the game. This aside, however, the basic objective of the Rueff proposal is the elimination of reserve currency holdings by monetary authorities. One obvious question is how to keep governments from holding reserve currencies instead of gold when there are so many advantages in holding reserves in the form of foreign exchange. Even if existing balances were liquidated with gold, what is to prevent their being built up again? One answer would be that the reserve currency countries should maintain balance of payments equilibrium. But even balance on the liquidity basis would not prevent the buildup of reserve currency balances *pari passu* with the accumulation of gold by the reserve currency country, or by shifts of reserve currency assets from foreign private holders to monetary authorities. More importantly, the Rueff proposal would eliminate the contribution of increased dollar liabilities to the supply of international reserves so that world reserves could expand only by increases in official gold holdings. Between the end of 1965 and March 1968, official gold holdings had declined by more than $4 billion.

The CRU Proposal for Stretching Gold Reserves

An alternative to increasing gold reserves by raising the price of gold is the Collective Reserve Unit (CRU) proposal, with the distribution of the CRUs linked directly to gold holdings. Under this scheme,[9] which was at one time proposed by France in the Group of Ten, members of a group of countries would each deposit a prescribed amount of gold with an agent who, in turn, would deposit an equal amount of gold with each member. The assets created by the deposits of gold with the agent would constitute the Collective Reserve Unit; and the gold deposited with the agent would be counted as a part of the member's gold reserves. CRUs would not be used directly for settlements between participants, but would be employed only on periodic settlement dates. Between

[9] There are several variants of the Collective Reserve Unit proposal, not all of which are linked to gold holdings.

settlement dates, the gold reserves of the participants would change in the normal course of international transactions. On settlement dates, there would be a restoration of a uniform ratio of CRUs to gold, so that participants losing gold during the period would regain a fraction of the gold they had lost while giving up CRUs, and participants gaining gold during the period would give up a fraction of the gold they had gained in exchange for CRUs. For example, suppose a country started out with $1 million in gold and $1 million in CRUs, and that during the period until the next settlement date it lost $500 thousand in gold so that it had $500 thousand in gold and $1 million in CRUs. If the proportion of gold to CRUs for the group as a whole were still one to one, the country in question should have $750 thousand in gold and $750 thousand in CRUs. In the reshuffle on the settlement date, the country would receive $250 thousand in gold from participants that had gained gold, and it would give up $250 thousand in CRUs.[10]

The United States and other governments opposed this variant of the CRU scheme because it puts a premium on holding gold as against other reserve assets—which is exactly what the French desired. Moreover, the arrangement would amount to a disguised increase in the price of gold, since gold holdings would be increased in value in proportion to the ratio of CRUs to gold provided under the scheme.[11]

Proposals to Replace Reserve Currency Holdings with a New Form of International Asset

Some economists have tended to agree with the French government's argument that official reserves should not take the form of reserve currencies and that additions to international liquidity should not take the form of increases in official holdings of reserve currencies generated by balance of payments deficits of reserve

[10] If the group as a whole had gained or lost gold, the uniform ratio of gold to CRUs would change. For a discussion of this proposal see Group of Ten, *Report of the Study Group on the Creation of Reserve Assets* (Rome: Bank of Italy, May 1965), pp. 26–29.

[11] *Ibid.*

currency countries. They hold that additions to world liquidity should take the form of newly created international reserve assets. They differ in their views regarding the future role of gold in the international monetary system, but they also disagree with the Rueff position that gold should be the sole, or even the principal, reserve asset.

The Triffin Plan

The position of Robert Triffin is somewhat unique in that, like Rueff, he would abolish official holdings of reserve currencies entirely, but, unlike Rueff, he would not have gold play a major role in the international monetary system. Reserves would consist of gold and a new form of international reserve asset—special deposits in the International Monetary Fund (XIMF deposits).[12] Triffin advances three arguments for his position. First, reserve currencies are vulnerable to conversion into gold and thus their volume may be subject to erratic changes. Second, the growth of international reserves should not depend upon haphazard shifts in the balance of payments of reserve currency countries; rather, a steady rise in international liquidity should be brought about in an orderly way through the creation of XIMF deposits. Third, Triffin sympathizes with the French and other European central bankers who object to financing the U.S. deficit by the expansion of foreign holdings of dollar balances. Under the present system, the alternative to not accumulating dollar balances would be a collapse of the international monetary system.[13]

According to the original Triffin Plan, members of the IMF would transfer their holdings of dollars and sterling to the IMF in exchange for XIMF deposits. The IMF would seek gradually to

[12] The Triffin Plan is outlined in Triffin's *Gold and the Dollar Crisis* (New Haven: Yale University Press, 1960). Triffin's more recent proposals are found in *Contingency Planning for U.S. International Monetary Policy*, Subcommittee on International Exchange and Payments, U.S. Congress, Joint Economic Committee (Washington, D.C.: USGPO, December 1966), pp. 133–144; and "The International Monetary System," *Moorgate and Wall Street*, Summer 1965.

[13] For a discussion of these points see Robert Triffin, "The Coexistence of Three Types of Reserve Assets," Banca Nazionale del Lavoro *Quarterly Review*, Rome, June 1967, pp. 107–134.

liquidate these dollar and sterling assets by requiring the United States and Britain to amortize them at a rate of 5 percent per annum, with payments made out of existing gold reserves and earned surpluses. It may be noted that at the end of 1967, U.S. liquid liabilities to foreign official institutions totaled $15.7 billion, while U.S. Treasury gold holdings were about $12.1 billion. Hence, under the Triffin Plan, the United States would be required to pay to the IMF over a twenty-year period an amount equal to all of its gold holdings (as of December 31, 1967) plus an additional $3.6 billion from earned surpluses. Since Britain's gold reserves are small compared with its sterling liabilities, that country would need to earn substantial surpluses in order to liquidate the sterling balances held by the IMF.

Under the Triffin Plan, the IMF would have the power to expand XIMF deposits through investments in domestic securities of member countries and in obligations of international agencies such as the World Bank, the investments being made in XIMF deposit credits. These operations would be similar to open market operations of a central bank in regulating the volume of domestic currency. The expansion of XIMF deposits would be sufficient to increase world reserves at some agreed rate, say 3 percent per year.

All members would be required to accept XIMF deposits in settlement of international obligations. However, they would need only to maintain XIMF deposits equal to 20 percent of their total reserves; the remaining 80 percent could be held in gold or "excess" XIMF deposits. They could, therefore, buy dollars with XIMF deposits and convert the dollars into gold. Under these circumstances, the United States might soon be drained of its remaining gold, and while XIMF deposits would not be convertible directly into gold, it is conceivable that XIMF deposits might depreciate in terms of gold unless the maximum percentage of XIMF deposits which IMF members are required to hold were raised substantially above the original 20 percent suggested by Triffin.[14]

In his more recent writings and statements, Triffin sees a dimin-

[14] For a criticism of the original Triffin Plan see Oscar L. Altman, "Professor Triffin on International Liquidity and the Role of the Fund," IMF *Staff Papers*, May 1961, pp. 161–191.

ishing role for gold and its eventual demonetization. Thus, he states that, "after agreement is reached on a new type of international reserve asset, gold will retain a gradually tapering off role in the system, until all countries have acquired sufficient familiarity with, and confidence in, the new reserve asset."[15] However, it is difficult to see how gold can be demonetized in the absence of a general agreement on the part of the major countries not to purchase gold and to accept and hold a large proportion of their reserves in the form of the new international asset. So long as the system provides for maintaining parity between gold and other reserve assets, there will be the constant danger that a preference for gold will undermine the value of other reserve assets.

Proposals to Supplement the Existing Reserves by a New Form of Reserve Asset

Unlike the Triffin Plan, most proposals in recent years have involved the creation of a new form of reserve asset which would *supplement* rather than *replace* existing reserve assets, including both gold and reserve currencies. Three broad categories of proposals for the creation of new reserve assets have been seriously considered. One group of proposals provides for a reserve asset to be created by a limited group of countries and distributed to this limited group for their use in the settlement of international balances. A second category of proposals provides for the creation of reserve units which would be distributed broadly among all countries or among all members of the IMF. Under the third category of proposals, the IMF would create deposits by making investments in international institutions or individual countries. This third category is similar to the Triffin Plan except that the reserve units would not replace reserve currency holdings. The first category of proposals may be divided into those that provide for the creation of a reserve unit outside the IMF and those that provide for the creation of reserve units within the IMF. The second and third categories of proposals generally provide for the creation of some kind of a reserve unit by or through the IMF.

[15] Triffin, "The Coexistence of Three Types of Reserve Assets," p. 128.

Collective Reserve Units—The Bernstein CRU Proposal[16]

Under the Bernstein CRU proposal, a limited group of countries, probably the Group of Ten, would deposit agreed amounts of their own currencies in a Reserve Unit Account in return for an equivalent amount of reserve units. For example, if the United States were allotted $500 million of reserve units, it would deposit an equivalent amount of dollars which would be guaranteed against depreciation. Bernstein suggests that the Reserve Unit Account might be established as a subsidiary of the IMF, but the account would be quite separate from the other assets and regular operations of the IMF. Allotments of reserve units to participating countries might be based on their proportionate quotas in the IMF or on some other basis that would reflect the relative importance of the participants. In this respect, the Bernstein proposal differs from the CRU proposal favored by the French, since in the latter reserve units would be allocated solely on the basis of the gold holdings of the participants. In other respects, however, the Bernstein proposal is similar to the gold-linked CRU proposal in that reserve units would be used in making settlements in a fixed relationship to gold. Thus, if the ratio of gold to reserve units were established at one to one, the country purchasing $100 million (equivalent) of the currency of another country with gold would deliver $50 million in gold and $50 million in reserve units.

Bernstein suggests that the participating members would determine the amount of reserve units to be issued each year with a view to assuring "the normal trend growth of aggregate reserves." Thus, he suggests that agreement might be reached on the annual issue for a period of five years ahead, but if for some reason the agreed amount to be issued in a given year should appear to be too large or too small, the actual issue could be increased or decreased by the participating countries. The appropriate amount of reserve

16 See Edward M. Bernstein, "Further Evolution of The International Monetary System," *Moorgate and Wall Street*, Summer 1965; see also Edward M. Bernstein, "The Bernstein Approach," in Randall Hinshaw (ed.), *Monetary Reform and the Price of Gold: Alternative Approaches* (Baltimore: Johns Hopkins Press, 1967), pp. 53–73.

units for assuring the desired growth of aggregate reserves would depend upon the movements of other reserve assets, including both gold and reserve currencies.

According to Bernstein, the reserve unit plan would not discourage participating countries from holding their reserves in other forms, either gold or foreign exchange, but would supplement existing reserve assets. Thus, if some countries held more reserve units than were required to match their gold holdings in making settlements, such countries would be free to lend or sell reserve units to countries with a deficiency; alternatively, they could request the IMF subsidiary serving as trustee for the Reserve Unit Account to convert reserve units into constituent currencies. Thus, in contrast to both the Triffin Plan and the CRU scheme linked with gold, the Bernstein CRU proposal would not discourage or outlaw the holding of official reserves in the form of reserve currencies.

The Roosa Plan—Fund Unit Account[17]

The plan of Robert Roosa, which was made public shortly after he resigned as Under Secretary of the U.S. Treasury Department, is of special interest since Roosa had a profound influence on the U.S. government's views on international monetary reform. Moreover, Roosa played a leading role in the deliberations of the Group of Ten during 1963 and 1964. The Roosa Plan provides for the contribution by a limited group of countries of their currencies to an account created within the IMF. In turn, each contributing country would receive a "checking account" in the Fund Unit Account which it could use to make payments to other monetary authorities or international financial institutions. Unlike the Bernstein CRU Plan, such transactions would in no way be tied to gold. Each contributing member would agree to accept Fund Units from any other monetary authority or international financial institution, at least up to the amount of its own contribution to the account.

The countries that would contribute to the account and receive initial allotments of Fund Units would be limited to those whose

[17] See Robert V. Roosa, *Monetary Reform for the World Economy* (New York: Harper and Row, 1965), pp. 75–100.

currencies were used for international transactions; the relative shares of contributions to the total account would reflect the use of a participant's currency as a reserve currency, including the drawings of that currency from the IMF over a preceding period.[18] The Fund Unit would be transferable among monetary authorities and international institutions throughout the world and might be used by any country as a part of its reserves. The volume of Fund Unit deposits, Roosa believes, should be determined by all members of the IMF and not just the countries eligible for contributing their own currencies and receiving the initial allotment of Fund Units. The reason for this is that the Fund Unit would be expected to have general acceptance and contribute to the total volume of international reserves, so that all members of the international community would have a stake in the determination of the volume of Fund Units. Roosa suggests that changes might be recommended by the Managing Director of the IMF or by a special committee of IMF governors, and that such recommendations could, in turn, be presented at the annual meetings of the IMF Board of Governors for debate and approval or rejection. Roosa apparently rejects any fixed formula for a steady growth of aggregate reserves as a basis for determining the volume of the Fund Units, and favors the managed approach which considers the need for reserves in the light of emerging circumstances.[19]

Proposals for the Creation of New Reserve Units to be Distributed Initially to All Members of the IMF

As might be expected, many representatives of the developing countries, as well as many economists in the developed countries, objected strongly to the creation of new reserve units which would add to the total volume of aggregate reserves, but which would be distributed to a limited number of developed countries, such as the Group of Ten. The Managing Director of the IMF, Pierre-Paul Schweitzer, also objected to any plan for the creation of interna-

---

[18] *Ibid.*, p. 81.

[19] *Ibid.*, p. 99. Roosa is careful to point out that the Fund Unit Account would only supplement and in no way supplant other reserve assets, including the expansion of reserve currency holdings.

tional liquidity which, in the first instance, would benefit only a handful of developed countries. The argument of those members of the Group of Ten who favored creation of a new reserve asset by and for a limited number of countries was that only the currencies of the financially strong countries would provide the real assets behind a new reserve unit. Moreover, it was believed that, rather than build up their reserves, the developing countries would quickly spend in the developed countries any additional reserves allotted to them. This position did not prevail in the plan for Special Drawing Rights which was finally adopted by the Group of Ten in August 1967 and approved by the Governors of the IMF at the annual meeting in Rio de Janeiro in September 1967. Before discussing the SDR proposal, we shall look briefly at some of the other proposals which provided for the allocation of newly created reserves to all IMF members.

The Angell Plan[20]

A number of economists who are in agreement with both the need for establishing a new international reserve asset and the desirability of having this asset created by the IMF are nevertheless critical of the Triffin Plan as regards both the manner in which the volume of XIMF reserve deposits would be increased and the roles of gold and of reserve currencies in the total composition of reserve assets. James Angell proposed an alternative scheme whereby the IMF would create transferable deposits distributed to each member of the Fund in accordance with its quota minus any net debt of the member to the Fund. Each member would be required to accept IMF deposits in settlement of claims or for the acquisition of that country's currency. Under the Triffin Plan, members would be required to hold no more than 20 percent of their total reserves in IMF deposits and the remainder in gold (since key currencies would no longer be held as reserves). Angell has objected that the Triffin Plan might soon exhaust the IMF holdings of gold since members could demand gold in exchange

[20] See James W. Angell, "The Organization of the International Monetary System: An Alternative Proposal," *Economic Journal*, December 1961, pp. 691–708.

for XIMF deposits held in excess of the minimum of 20 percent of the members' reserves.[21] Angell wanted to replace gold with IMF deposits; no member could require gold payment from any other member for the purchase of its currency. The IMF could expand its transferable deposits by purchasing gold or by buying other currencies. Limits would be established on the IMF's holdings of member currencies and such limits would, in effect, determine the total volume of IMF deposits (plus the initial IMF deposits issued in accordance with IMF quotas plus whatever amount of gold was purchased by the IMF). Under the Angell Plan, gold would be relegated to a minor role and probably would not be used in the settlement of international balances.

The Angell Plan raises the question of what volume of IMF deposits a country could realistically be required to accept from other countries. Triffin's 20 percent formula has been widely regarded as unfeasible given the strong preference for gold, but it is feared that Angell's proposal might be unacceptable to many surplus developed countries. This question will be discussed further when we take up the IMF's new SDR facility.

The Stamp Plan

An important provision of the Triffin Plan is that a portion of the new XIMF credits would be used for investment in international assistance agencies, thus channeling the newly created reserves initially to the developing countries for financing imports required by their development programs. Two other proposals employ this principle—namely the Stamp Plan and the proposal of a group of experts appointed by the Secretary General of the United Nations Conference on Trade and Development (UNCTAD). According to the plan proposed by Maxwell Stamp,[22] the Fund would be permitted to create credit by issuing certificates which member countries would agree to accept in settlement of international obligations up to the amount of their quotas, and to hold as a part of their reserves. The Fund would lend the certificates to

---

[21] They would first convert excess XIMF deposits into dollars and then convert the dollars into gold.

[22] Maxwell Stamp, "The Stamp Plan—1966 Version," *Moorgate and Wall Street*, Autumn, 1962.

the International Development Association (IDA). IDA would lend in a normal way, but as currencies were required for the purchase of imports by the borrowers, the certificates would be presented to the exporting countries in exchange for their currencies. A country might decide that it did not want to convert certificates into its currency for financing IDA loans to be spent within its economy. However, that country would be required to accept the certificates from third countries that needed its currency for dealing with balance of payments deficits.

The UNCTAD Experts' Group Proposal

Representatives of developing countries have followed closely the discussions and the reports of the Group of Ten and have expressed considerable concern about the possible adoption of a new reserve asset which would be created by and for a limited group of developed countries. The issue was discussed at the 1964 UNCTAD conference in Geneva, and in accordance with a conference resolution, a group of experts was appointed by Raul Prebisch, Secretary General of UNCTAD, to make a study on international monetary issues with particular attention to the needs of the developing countries. The UNCTAD experts' report on *International Monetary Issues and the Developing Countries,* issued in October 1965,[23] reviewed the major proposals under discussion at that time and put forward a proposal combining the elements of those plans which appeared to give the most to the developing countries.

The UNCTAD experts' proposal rejected those plans which limited distribution of new reserve assets to a few developed countries. The experts pointed out that developing countries were greatly in need of additional reserves, and they were critical of the view that the new reserve facility should be distributed only to those countries whose currencies provide the effective backing for the new reserve unit. In essence, the experts proposed that (1) Fund units be issued to all members against currencies contributed by IMF members in accordance with an agreed formula, e.g., on the basis of IMF quotas; (2) a portion of the currencies

[23] New York: United Nations (Sales No.: 66II.D.2.), 1966.

acquired by the Fund from the developed countries in exchange for the Fund Units should be invested in IBRD bonds. Thus, the UNCTAD experts' proposal combined the idea of a new Fund unit backed by the currencies of all members and distributed to all members with that of the Triffin Plan, according to which additions to international liquidity would in the first instance be employed to finance economic development.

The idea of a link between reserve creation and development financing has been strongly opposed not only by many central bankers but also by other financial specialists who believe that decisions regarding the amount of liquidity required for the optimum performance of the international monetary system should not be influenced by the need for development financing. A final objection to the UNCTAD experts' proposal is that unless all of the currency of a particular developed country used to purchase IBRD bonds was spent in that country, that country would not receive its proportionate (net) share of the reserve creation. Assume, for example, that the United States receives $1 billion in Fund units, and that the equivalent amount of dollars paid into the Fund was used to buy IBRD bonds. If only $500 million were used by the recipients of the IBRD loans for expenditures in the United States and the remainder used to make purchases in Western European countries, the U.S. net reserve position would profit by only $500 million.[24]

The IMF Managing Director's Proposals

The IMF has participated actively in the discussions on possible changes in the international monetary system. It has been represented in the study groups and discussions of the Group of Ten, and the IMF staff has made studies of the need for international liquidity and has analyzed various proposals for supplementing international reserves. In 1966, the Managing Director of the IMF, Pierre-Paul Schweitzer, put forth two proposals of his own.[25]

[24] The $500 million accruing to European countries would represent an increase in U.S. liquid dollar liabilities, and a portion of these might be used to acquire gold or other reserve assets of the United States.

[25] *International Monetary Fund 1966 Annual Report* (Washington, D.C., 1966), pp. 18–20.

The principal responsibility of the IMF in the field of liquidity has been the provision of "conditional liquidity"—that is, the Fund stands prepared to provide the credits, repayable within three to five years, to its members in need of financing to cover balance of payments deficits. Until recently, at least, the IMF has not advocated an increase in unconditional liquidity, but it has been concerned about the adequacy of its resources for providing conditional liquidity. For example, in its *1965 Annual Report* (p. 15), the Fund stated that, "ideally, countries' needs for additional liquidity could be met by adequate increases in conditional liquidity." However, the IMF did admit that a time might come when additions to the world's supply of unconditional liquidity might be desirable, and its *1965 Annual Report* also suggested mechanisms by which the supply of unconditional liquidity might be expanded through the IMF.[26]

It is not surprising that the Managing Director and staff of the IMF would view with some concern proposals for expanding international liquidity through the creation of reserve assets by a limited number of countries outside the Fund. Not only does the Fund believe that it has a special responsibility for the volume and method of creation of international liquidity, but that "reserve creation is the concern of all member countries, and . . . all should participate, with due safeguards, both in the distribution of newly created reserves and in the decisions which lead to their creation, and that such creation should take place either through the Fund or through an affiliate of the Fund."[27]

In 1966, the Managing Director of the Fund put forth two proposals for the creation of additional reserve assets in accordance with the principles noted above. The first would consist of an increase in automatic drawing rights of members without their having to subscribe additional amounts of gold. There are, however, limits to the expansion of automatic drawing rights since the IMF would have the obligation to supply whatever currency the member utilizing the drawing right would demand for purposes of settling

[26] *International Monetary Fund 1965 Annual Report* (Washington, D.C., 1965), pp. 38–39.
[27] *International Monetary Fund 1966 Annual Report*, p. 19.

current deficits. If the IMF's supply of the currencies demanded and of the gold with which to buy them were exhausted, it could not meet this obligation. The second proposal was for the issuance of reserve units by an affiliate of the Fund, membership in which would be open to all Fund members. In this case, Fund reserve units would be directly transferable among members, but members would be permitted to use the new reserve units only for settling deficits. Under the second scheme, surplus countries would be obligated to accept Fund reserve units in exchange for their own currencies, but this obligation would be limited to, say, three times the cumulative amount of reserve units issued to each country.[28] In both schemes, the creation of additional reserves would be the subject of international decision at intervals of, say, five years. It is worth noting that the scheme finally adopted by the Group of Ten and the Board of Governors of the IMF in 1967 drew heavily on the Managing Director's proposal.

Proposals to Demonetize Gold

Growing recognition of the incompatibility between reserve currencies and gold, as reserve assets which countries are free to hold at their option, has led to two types of responses. The first type is represented by Triffin and Rueff, who have made differing proposals for eliminating key currencies as reserve assets; the second is represented by those who would demonetize gold in favor of reserve currencies or reserve currencies plus some form of newly created reserve unit.

There are two general approaches to the demonetization of gold as an international reserve asset. The first, which might be called the Gresham's Law approach, would involve agreement among countries not to require gold payment for settling balances or for the purchase of a country's currency. For example, members of the IMF could acquire the foreign currencies they need by purchases with IMF reserve units, and all member countries would be required to accept IMF units in exchange for their own cur-

[28] *Ibid.*, p. 20.

rency from the IMF or from other members.[29] While gold would also be acceptable for the same purposes, countries might prefer to use IMF reserve units or reserve currencies (maintained at parity with IMF reserve units) rather than gold in international transactions, unless the price of gold declined on the free markets below $35 per ounce. But whatever happened to its price, gold would gradually be displaced by other reserve assets, especially since the supply of gold would grow slowly relative to the growth of total reserve assets. In addition, the industrial demand for gold, which is growing rapidly, might gradually absorb both the new production of gold and the existing monetary supply as well.

The other approach to gold demonetization would be for monetary authorities (or the United States alone) to agree not to purchase gold at $35 per ounce, or possibly to reduce the price at which gold would be purchased below the gold parity.[30] In the absence of unlimited monetary demand for gold at a fixed price, the price of gold could be driven down to a level which represented equilibrium between the demand by industry and private hoarders and the supply from new production. Once people were convinced that an ounce of gold could no longer be counted on to acquire $35 (or the equivalent in other convertible currencies) but that it might in the future be worth less in terms of these currencies, speculative and hoarding demand would rapidly decline, and gold would be purchased and sold simply as a commodity like silver or other precious metals.

A growing number of economists and bankers now appear to agree that, in one way or another, gold will eventually be demonetized or largely replaced by other reserve media. A step in this direction was taken by the members of the London gold pool in

[29] This is essentially the provision of the Angell Plan described above.

[30] Some economists believe that the United States could effect a reduction in the world price of gold. See "Statement Submitted by Professor Emile Despres," in *New Approach to United States International Economic Policy*, Hearings before the Subcommittee on International Exchange and Payments, U.S. Congress, Joint Economic Committee, 89th Cong., 2nd sess., September 9, 1966, pp. 39–42; see also Emile Despres, Charles P. Kindleberger, and Walter S. Salant, "The Dollar and World Liquidity: A Minority View," *The (London) Economist*, February 5, 1966, pp. 526–529. Others believe that this would require joint action by the monetary authorities of the major countries.

their statement of March 17, 1968, terminating the operations of the pool.[31] According to this statement, it was decided that gold would no longer be supplied to the London gold market or to any other gold market. Moreover, since the existing stock of monetary gold was deemed sufficient (in view of the prospective establishment of the facility for Special Drawing Rights), it was decided that the purchase of gold from the private market, including new gold production, would no longer be necessary. Finally, it was agreed that henceforth they would not sell gold to monetary authorities to replace gold sold in private markets.

If at some future time the leading monetary authorities were to agree not to change the ratio of their gold holdings to total reserve assets by demanding gold from the United States, or if the United States were to place further limits on its willingness to sell gold against dollars, the role of gold in settling international balances would tend to disappear in favor of SDRs and reserve currencies. The possible future role of gold will be discussed further in the concluding chapter.

Proposals for Flexible Exchange Rates

A number of economists would replace the present international monetary system based on fixed exchange parities (with provision for periodic changes in gold parities after consultation with the IMF) with a system of flexible exchange rates.[32] Since the present system recognizes that balance of payments equilibrium may be incompatible with domestic objectives at existing exchange rates and that exchange rate adjustment should be made in the case of a fundamental disequilibrium, the argument for flexible rates in contrast with the present system is one that favors actual or poten-

[31] The members of the London gold pool were Belgium, Germany, Italy, the Netherlands, Switzerland, the United Kingdom, and the United States. For the text of the statement, see Appendix B.

[32] See, for example, Milton Friedman, "The Case for Flexible Exchange Rates," *Essays in Positive Economics* (Chicago: University of Chicago Press, 1953); Egon Sohmen, *Fluctuating Exchange Rates: Theory and Controversy* (Chicago: University of Chicago Press, 1961); J. E. Meade, *The Balance of Payments* (London: Oxford University Press, 1955).

tial flexibility in accordance with free market forces as against periodic adjustment of rates subject to some form of market intervention.

Those favoring flexible rates point out that flexibility is not the same as instability. When based on monetary and fiscal policies designed to avoid instability, flexible rates need not be subject to fluctuation. But by pegging rates through market intervention, monetary authorities can delay or avoid taking the appropriate internal monetary actions necessary for the maintenance of stability. With flexible rates, the weakening of a currency in the exchange market becomes a signal for the need to take appropriate monetary action. Moreover, flexible rates are an alternative to direct controls which countries are frequently led to impose with respect to either current trade or capital movements in place of more fundamental policy changes. Since balance of payments equilibrium at fixed exchange rates is often incompatible with high levels of output and employment, exchange rates should be permitted to fluctuate as an alternative to controls.

Critics of a flexible rate system point out that exchange rates are subject to temporary forces arising from seasonal and cyclical movements in demand and supply and from speculative movements which may soon be reversed. It is argued that to permit exchange rates to fluctuate in response to these forces would create harmful and needless uncertainties for traders and investors and would impair world trade and capital movements. In answer to these criticisms, those favoring a flexible rate system argue that by letting rates react to temporary forces tending to depress the value of a currency, the fall in the value of the currency will quickly terminate or reverse such movements with perhaps only a modest change in the exchange rate. But so long as a currency under pressure is pegged and its value is believed likely to move in only one direction (downward), speculation against that currency may continue without danger of loss to the speculators. However, if the exchange rate is permitted to adjust to pressures against it, the extent of the decline in the rate is limited by the fact that traders and speculators may have to pay more for the currency in the future. Some economists favoring flexible rates also point out that forces tending to depress a currency can be offset by an increase in interest rates so as to attract short-term capital. But if countries were to adopt internal measures to maintain exchange rate stability in the face of all external forces tending to depress the exchange value of their currency, they would be subject to much more severe constraints on their internal monetary policies than they would be under a fixed rate system.

We may discern two conflicting arguments for exchange flexibility. One group of economists sees flexibility as imposing a severe discipline on monetary authorities in order to maintain exchange rate stability. Another group sees flexibility as a means of balance of payments adjustment which does not require interference with domestic policy goals. Still other proponents of flexible exchange rates appear to take a dual position. On the one hand, they see definite advantages in forcing countries to realize the consequences of their internal policies without obscuring them, either by the imposition of exchange controls or by prolonged deficit financing. On the other hand, they see advantages in enabling countries to adjust their balance of payments readily without interference with domestic policies.

Perhaps the strongest argument in favor of flexibility is that such a system avoids the use of trade and exchange controls for balance of payments purposes. However, exchange rate flexibility will not enable a country to dispense with internal monetary discipline. As has already been noted, an improvement in the current account usually cannot take place without a reduction of domestic spending relative to output. A change in the exchange rate only facilitates balance of payments *adjustment*; it does not guarantee *improvement* in the balance. A policy of flexible exchange rates in the absence of any effort to reduce spending is likely to lead to hyperinflation, with the external depreciation of the currency feeding the internal depreciation until the entire payments mechanism breaks down.

Whatever the outcome of the arguments for and against flexible rates, they do not constitute a feasible alternative for the United States, and probably not for Britain either if that country desires to maintain a reserve currency status. Flexible rates would also appear to be incompatible with membership in a common market, such as the European Economic Community, since reasonable stability of competitive conditions is essential for countries seeking to merge their economies. Exchange rate flexibility between the currencies of different blocks of countries (with stable rates among the countries within the same bloc) is conceivable; such a system existed during the 1930's.

The "Band" Proposal

A compromise between the present system of fixed exchange rates and a system of flexible rates is provided by the "band" proposal which at one time or another has been advocated by quite a number of economists. Essentially, it is proposed that the permitted margin of fluctuations in exchange rates above and below parity be broadened from the 1 percent stipulated in the Fund Agreement to several percentage points. Thus, if a currency were permitted to fluctuate freely by 5 percent on either side of a parity, it could move within a range of 10 percent without a change in the par value. It is argued that such a range would provide considerable scope for changes in relative prices among countries, which in turn would help to achieve an adjustment of the trade balance for deficit countries.[33] It is also argued that a widening of the permissable variation of exchange rates would tend to dampen capital movements in response to differences in interest rates.

Assume, for example, that in a given country interest rates fall relative to rates abroad. An outflow of capital from this country to countries with higher interest rates would raise the spot price of foreign exchange relative to the forward rate. The wider the spread between the forward and spot rates, the greater the cost of hedging; hence, capital flow induced by the interest rate differ-

[33] For an excellent description of the history of the "band" proposal and a presentation of the arguments for and against the proposal, see George N. Halm, *The "Band" Proposal: The Limits of Permissible Exchange Rate Variations* (Princeton, N.J.: International Finance Section, Princeton University, January 1965).

ential would be retarded.[34] Uncovered speculation against the currency might also be discouraged, since speculators would be subject to a greater risk from a sudden rise in the exchange value of that currency as a consequence of either a shift in the balance of payments or intervention on the part of the monetary authorities. However, the question of whether the existence of a wider range of fluctuation in the exchange rate would provide an advantage to the monetary authorities in defending a currency against bear speculation has been the subject of considerable debate in the literature.[35]

The advantage of the "band" proposal over unlimited flexibility of exchange rates appears to arise mainly from the belief that governments would not be willing to accept a system of flexible rates but might be induced to accept a system of wider variations from parity than that established by the Fund Agreement. The arrangement provides a range within which central banks might be willing to permit market forces to operate and thereby produce adjustments through the price mechanism.

In general, those economists who favor flexible rates as a kind of discipline to force monetary authorities to take appropriate internal monetary and fiscal measures in order to avoid a depreciation of their currency have not favored the "band" proposal.[36] On the other hand, those economists who regard exchange rate flexibility as a desirable means of adjusting the balance of payments have tended to favor the "band" proposal as a workable compromise between fixed rates and unlimited exchange rate flexibility.

---

[34] Much would depend upon the behavior of the forward rate, since speculative factors might raise the forward rate with the spot rate so as to prevent a wider spread between the two rates.

[35] See Leland B. Yeager, "A Skeptical View of the 'Band' Proposal," *The National Banking Review*, IV (March 1967), 291–297; Henry N. Goldstein, "A Further Comment on an Aspect of the 'Band' Proposal," *The National Banking Review*, IV (June 1967), 511–513; and E. Ray Canterbery, "A Skeptical View of the 'Band' Proposal: A Comment," *The National Banking Review*, IV (June 1967), 514–516.

[36] For example, this is the position taken by Leland Yeager in opposing the "band" proposal. Yeager, "A Skeptical View of the 'Band' Proposal," pp. 291–297.

The Crawling Peg

Still another compromise between fixed and flexible exchange rates is provided by the proposal of Professor James Meade and others which has been called the "crawling peg."[37] According to this proposal a country in disequilibrium would depreciate its currency gradually at a rate of 2 percent per year so as to avoid a sharp fluctuation which might interfere with trade. Changes in parities, either upward or downward, would be gradual and predictable. It is believed that such changes would be more readily acceptable by the public and would create less political difficulties for the government undertaking a devaluation. To prevent speculative withdrawal of funds from a country undergoing gradual devaluation, it is suggested that the interest rate differential between the devaluing country and other major countries not undergoing devaluation would be sufficient to compensate for the loss in the exchange value of the devaluing currency. Thus, during the period of gradual devaluation at the rate of 2 percent per annum, interest rates in the devaluing country should be 2 percent above those in the major financial centers of the rest of the world. One objection to this proposal would be that a devaluing country would have to follow an interest rate policy which might differ from that dictated by domestic objectives.

The IMF Special Drawing Rights (SDR) Facility

The plan for reserve creation adopted in September 1967 at the annual meeting of the IMF Board of Governors at Rio de Janeiro embodied the results of some four years of study and negotiation in the Group of Ten. However, the deliberations on the plan that was finally agreed upon by the Group of Ten in August 1967 were influenced by a much broader forum, including the staff and executive directors of the IMF and private and government economists

---

[37] See James E. Meade, "The International Monetary Mechanism," *The Three Banks Review*, September 1964, pp. 3–25; see also John H. Williamson, *The Crawling Peg* (Princeton, N.J.: International Finance Section, Princeton University, December 1965).

throughout the world. Few issues have generated as much discussion and writing among professional economists, bankers, and government officials. Like most agreements involving controversial questions, the plan for the creation of SDRs in the Fund represents a compromise; the new reserve facility embodies the elements of several approaches to the creation of additional international liquidity. Although we have undoubtedly not seen the final form which the future international monetary system may take, it appears likely that the SDR plan (which had not, at the time of writing, been finally approved by members of the IMF) will play an important role in the emerging international payments mechanism.

Outline of the SDR Plan

The following paragraphs summarize the more important provisions of the SDR plan.[38]

1. An amendment to the Articles of Agreement of the IMF will establish a Special Drawing Rights Account, the operations and resources of which will be separate from the regular operations and resources of the IMF referred to as the General Account. The General Account will be authorized to hold and use SDRs.

2. Participation in the SDR plan will be open to any member of the IMF that undertakes the obligations of the amendment as outlined below. Allocation of drawing rights among members will be proportional to their existing IMF quotas. However, any member may refuse to participate in any or all SDR allotments.

3. Proposals for the establishment of drawing rights during a base period (normally five years) and the amount and rate at which drawings may be made, will be initiated by the Managing Director of the IMF, subject to approval by an 85 percent majority of the voting power of the participants.

4. Participants will be entitled to use SDRs to acquire an equivalent amount of a convertible currency either directly from another participant or through the Special Drawing Rights Account by transferring an amount of its holdings of SDRs. Partici-

[38] An analysis and interpretation of the proposed amendment to the IMF Articles of Agreement for establishing the SDR facility is given in Appendix A.

pants will be expected to use their drawing rights only for balance of payments needs or in the light of developments in its total reserves and not for the sole purpose of changing the composition of its reserves. The use of Special Drawing Rights will not be subject to prior challenge, but the Fund may make representations to any participant which the Fund believes has failed to observe these conditions and may direct drawings to such participants to the extent of such failure. (By directing drawings to countries that have sought to employ drawing rights in place of using their own reserves in order to change the composition of their reserve, the Fund could reconstitute the initial proportion of SDRs in their total reserve holdings.)

5. A participant's obligation to provide its currency against transfers of drawing rights will be limited to the point at which its total holdings of drawing rights equal three times its initial allocation. However, a participant may agree to hold drawing rights in excess of this limit.

6. Normally, currencies will be acquired from participants that have a strong balance of payments and reserve position. But this will not preclude the possibility that currencies will be acquired from participants with strong reserve positions even though they have moderate balance of payments deficits.

7. Members using their SDRs will have an obligation to reconstitute their position according to regulations established by the Fund. The rules for reconstitution of drawings made during the first basic period will be based on the following principles: (a) the average net use of a participant's special drawing rights, taking into account both use below and holdings above its net cumulative allocation, calculated on the basis of the preceding five years, shall not exceed 70 percent of its average net cumulative allocation during this period; and (b) participants will pay due regard to the desirability of pursuing, over time, a balanced relationship between their holdings of special drawing rights and other reserves.

8. Interest will be paid in SDRs on holdings of SDRs above the initial allocation. The cost of this interest would be assessed against participants in proportion to their allocations of drawing rights.

9. Subject to the provisions of (4) above, a participant may use its drawing rights to purchase balances of its own currency held by another participant, with the agreement of the latter.

10. The rights and obligations of participants and of the Special Drawing Account will be subject to an absolute maintenance of gold value.

The final form of the proposed amendment to the IMF Agreement that will bring into operation the new SDR facility was prepared by the IMF and released in April 1968. (See Appendix A.) In addition to conditions for the establishment of the SDR facility, the amendment provides for certain other changes in the Articles of Agreement of the IMF, including changes in the voting majorities required for important Fund decisions, the formal status of drawing rights in the Fund, and the requirements for repurchase.[39]

The European Economic Community countries have taken the position that, as a condition for ratifying the SDR plan, the Articles of Agreement of the IMF should be amended to require an 85 percent majority of the voting power, as opposed to the present 80 percent, for approval of future increases in IMF quotas. Since the EEC countries together have about 16 percent of the voting power in the IMF, an 85 percent majority requirement would give them an effective veto over increases in IMF quotas.[40] This change in voting power has been included in the proposed amendment. France has also taken the position that the new SDR

[39] Except for the changes in voting and those relating to the SDR plan itself, the proposed amendments do not fundamentally alter the present procedures and operations of the IMF.

[40] In a report of a subcommittee of the Joint Economic Committee of the Congress, it was recommended that the United States insist that the quotas of the Common Market countries be raised by an amount which would raise the voting power of the EEC countries to at least 20 percent of the total instead of changing the Articles of Agreement to require an 85 percent majority of the voting power for approval of an increase in quotas. Such an increase in the quotas of the EEC countries would require them to contribute additional currencies and gold to the IMF, a contribution which is believed to be in line with the international reserve position and obligations of these countries. See U.S. Congress, Joint Economic Committee, *Guidelines for Improving the International Monetary System—Round 2*, Report of the Subcommittee on International Exchange and Payments, U.S. Congress, Joint Economic Committee (Washington, D.C.: USGPO, December 19, 1967), p. 7.

plan should not be activated until the reserve currency countries (United States and Britain) have eliminated their balance of payments deficits. While the United States has accepted the change in the rules with respect to voting on increases in IMF quotas, it has opposed conditioning activation of the plan on the elimination of the deficit of any particular country. At a meeting of the Group of Ten (March 29–30, 1968) in Stockholm, Sweden, all members except France agreed to support the amendment to the IMF which would permit the activation of the new SDR facility (subject to approval by an 85 percent majority of the voting power of any specific SDR allocation proposed by the Managing Director of the IMF) at an early date. France refused to support the amendment on the grounds that the U.S. balance of payments was still in deficit.[41]

Analysis of the SDR Plan

Certain distinctive features of the SDR reserve facility may be emphasized in contrast with other proposals previously considered by the Group of Ten. First, the plan allocated the newly created reserves to *all* IMF members in proportion to their IMF quotas rather than allocating reserves among a limited number of individual countries. While the Group of Ten had initially favored a plan under which reserves would be created by and for the members of the Group of Ten plus a few additional countries, pressure from the IMF Managing Director and from countries outside the Group of Ten forced abandonment of this plan. It will be recalled that at one point the United States favored the creation of two types of reserve assets—one which would involve the establishment of automatic drawing rights in the IMF to be allocated among all members, and another which would take the form of a collective reserve unit created by and for a small group of countries.

While the SDRs constitute a form of unconditional liquidity, they retain certain characteristics of credit facilities normally made available by the IMF. For one thing, they are normally to be

[41] For the text of *Communiqué of the Ministerial Meeting of the Group of Ten*, March 29–30, 1968, Stockholm, Sweden, see International Monetary Fund, *International Financial News Survey*, April 5, 1968, p. 1.

used only in the event of a balance of payments deficit. This limitation is necessary to prevent countries from using SDRs in lieu of other reserve assets, and thereby changing the composition of their reserves, for instance, in favor of a larger proportion of gold holdings. Second, and more significant, however, is the requirement that members are not to use their allotment of drawing rights to exceed 70 percent of their net accumulated holdings over a five-year period. This requirement may, to a limited degree, impair the reserve quality of the SDRs.

Third, and a possible weakness of the SDR as a reserve asset, the obligation of members to accept SDRs in exchange for their own currency is limited to an amount equal to double the amount of their allocation, i.e., their total holdings of SDRs need not exceed three times their allocation. Once a country has reached this limit and prefers not to accept additional SDRs, other countries desiring to exchange SDRs for convertible currencies must acquire them from countries whose holdings of SDRs have not reached this limit (or who are willing to exceed the limit). Since the currencies sought are interconvertible, this should normally make little difference. Conceivably, however, the bulk of the convertible currency countries might have deficits, and all of these deficits might be concentrated on two or three surplus countries whose currencies would be in heavy demand. This situation could give rise to the scarce-currency problem envisaged in Article VII of the IMF Agreement providing for the rationing of scarce currencies. So long as the IMF had gold, it could purchase the currencies demanded since members have an unlimited obligation to sell their currencies to the Fund against gold. But the Fund's holdings of gold will in time constitute only a small percentage of accumulated SDRs.

A further difficulty might arise if several surplus countries were to elect not to participate in allocations of SDRs and hence avoid the obligation to accept them. This would signal a failure of cooperation without which no international monetary system could be successful.

Finally, a possible shortcoming of the SDR plan lies in the method of expanding the volume of SDRs. It has been apparent for some time that the views of governments and central bankers differ sharply on the question of the world's need for additional liquidity. The French government and the central bankers of certain other European countries have expressed the fear that even the present volume of international liquidity may be too large and that further additions would contribute to world inflation. Since 15 percent of the voting power of the IMF could veto a proposal to increase allotments of SDRs (or condition any agreement for their expansion on the attainment of U.S. balance of payments equilibrium), there can be no assurance that the new facility will provide what the majority of the nations of the world would regard as an adequate rate of growth in liquidity. This situation could be avoided by giving to the Managing Director of the IMF the power to expand SDRs at a maximum rate of, say, 3 percent per annum, with additional amounts being subject to approval by 85 percent of the voting power of the members. Such a delegation of power to the Managing Director would, of course, require an 85 percent majority vote.

Relationship of SDRs to Other Reserve Assets

In contrast to some of the other proposals for monetary reform which have been discussed in this chapter, SDRs are not designed to replace other reserve assets, but rather to supplement existing reserves. SDRs and reserve currencies would be interconvertible either directly or indirectly.[42] The relationship between reserve currencies and gold would remain the same so long as the United States continued to sell gold against dollars at $35 per ounce. The SDR plan does provide some safeguards against SDRs being used to increase the proportion of a member's other reserve assets relative to SDRs, but this would not seem to prevent members from increasing the proportion of SDRs plus gold in relation to reserve currencies. In time, SDRs might prove to be quite attractive as reserve assets compared with either gold or reserve currencies, since

[42] If a member wanted to convert a reserve currency into drawing rights, it could buy drawing rights from another country willing to sell them; alternatively, it could first acquire a currency eligible for repurchase by the General Account of the IMF and exchange that currency for a drawing right in the IMF.

SDRs have the double advantage of paying interest and of bearing an absolute gold value guarantee. (The absolute gold value guarantee would hold even if all of the IMF members voted to make a uniform change in their gold parities.)

If the United States should cease to buy gold as a consequence of heavy gold drains, the relationship between gold and reserve currencies would be broken. The United States could support the exchange value of the dollar by buying other convertible currencies with SDRs or with gold. If the United States exhausted its supply of both SDRs and gold along with its borrowing power in the IMF, the exchange value of the dollar would be determined by the willingness of other countries to support the dollar in order to avoid an appreciation of their own currencies. While such a dilemma is conceivable, it is highly unlikely that the major countries of the world would permit such a threat to the international monetary system; the problem would probably be dealt with through special measures of international monetary cooperation.

While the gold value guarantee would provide some advantage in holding SDRs as against reserve currencies, SDRs would by no means replace reserve currencies. Reserve currencies would be required as a means of payment and as a liquidity reserve for banks, corporations, and individuals engaged in international business. Moreover, since shifting between SDRs and reserve currencies would not be costless, governments and central banks would also need to maintain reserve currency balances. Therefore, both governments and private entities would need to maintain balances in reserve currencies. In addition, the modest interest proposed to be paid on SDR holdings would undoubtedly be substantially lower than the rates of return on liquid assets held in reserve currency countries. It has been suggested that interest paid on SDRs held in excess of a member's allotment would be 1½ percent.[43]

Criticisms of the SDR System

As might be expected, the SDR plan has come under attack from economists holding a variety of views on international mone-

[43] Statement by Pierre-Paul Schweitzer, Managing Director of the IMF. See *International Financial News Survey*, May 3, 1968, pp. 137–139.

tary reform. Most of the criticism is based on the fact that the SDR facility does not deal with many of the basic shortcomings of the present international system, such as the danger of a speculative conversion of foreign dollar holdings into gold or the inefficiency of the balance of payments adjustment process. The SDR plan deals mainly with the problem of providing an adequate volume of international reserve. However, some economists like Robert Triffin, who have been strong advocates of a plan for regulating the volume of international reserves, point to the weaknesses of the SDR plan—as embodied in the Proposed Amendment to the Articles of Agreement of the IMF—as a means of assuring an adequate volume of international reserves. Whether the SDR arrangement will be employed to offset reductions in reserves resulting from the withdrawal of reserve currencies and whether it will provide for a steady increase in the volume of international reserves depends on the willingness of IMF members holding 85 percent of the voting power of the Fund to support the necessary increases in SDR allocations; this is by no means assured.[44]

In general, two groups of economists, representing quite different views regarding the international monetary system, have either opposed the SDR plan or have been lukewarm to it. First, those who favor a flexible exchange rate approach have, as a rule, denied the need for any new supplement to international reserves. Arrangements for enabling countries to finance continued deficits through the creation of international reserves would, according to the flexible rate group, simply delay the making of fundamental adjustments, either by a change in exchange rates or through internal adjustments. On the other hand, those who favor exchange rate stability believe such stability should be achieved through appropriate domestic monetary and fiscal measures, and they do not regard the SDR scheme as making any significant contribution to the adjustment process. Still others have been unenthusiastic about

[44] For a discussion of the shortcomings of the SDR plan, see Robert Triffin, "The International Monetary Problem After Rio," *New Plan for International Monetary Reserves, Part II—Rio Monetary Agreement*, Hearings before the Subcommittee on International Exchange and Payments, U.S. Congress, Joint Economic Committee, 90th Cong., 1st sess. (Washington, D.C.: USGPO, 1967), pp. 128–135.

the SDR system for fear that it will undermine the world banker role of the United States. They prefer a definite break with gold and international cooperation based on the holding of key currencies, particularly the dollar, by central banks.

At the time of writing, there have been few outright attacks on the SDR plan, although there have been many criticisms of its inadequacy and many suggestions for improvement. A notable exception is Eugene Birnbaum, who has attacked the SDR scheme as a misguided plan to destroy the monetary role of gold and a departure from the Bretton Woods system as he interprets it. Birnbaum advocates a change in the system of dollar convertibility into gold to what he calls "current-account convertibility." Under "current-account convertibility" the United States would no longer convert dollars directly into gold but would convert dollars presented by central banks into the offering country's own currency. This is one of the methods of maintaining convertibility provided in the Articles of Agreement of the IMF. Alternatively, the United States could intervene directly in the foreign exchange market to maintain the exchange value of the dollar. The United States could obtain foreign currencies from the Fund either through purchase with gold or by drawing on the Fund. Birnbaum suggests that if the Fund's holdings of certain convertible currencies and of gold with which to purchase them were low, the Fund should borrow the currencies needed. Furthermore, if the Fund should decide that the policies of a surplus country whose currency was scarce were responsible for its chronic balance of payments surplus, it would offer the country the choice of either lending its currency to the Fund or having its currency formally declared to be scarce. Under Article VII of the IMF Agreement, other IMF members could then discriminate against purchases of the exports of that country.[45]

It appears that Birnbaum may be reading too much into the SDR facility. In itself it does not "destroy" the monetary role of gold; it simply provides a supplement to existing international reserves just as does the gold tranche established by the IMF. In fact,

---

[45] See Eugene A. Birnbaum, *Gold and the International Monetary System: An Orderly Reform*, Essays in International Finance (Princeton, N.J.: International Finance Section, Princeton University, April 1968), pp. 44–45.

much of what is accomplished by the SDR could have been accomplished by increasing the gold tranche of each member without requiring additional gold deposits. Hence, the SDR system might well be regarded as simply an extension of the Bretton Woods system itself.

It seems clear that the SDR plan must be judged on the basis of (a) whether a supplement to the present system of international currency reserves is required, and (b) whether the SDR arrangement will operate to provide an "adequate" volume of international reserves. Other shortcomings of the international monetary system will have to be dealt with by other measures.

The Future of the International Monetary System: Outlook and Conclusions

THE INTERNATIONAL MONETARY SYSTEM is undergoing such rapid transformation that it would be presumptuous to forecast its character even in the near future. Nevertheless, we can discern certain tendencies from recent events which, in the absence of unforeseen crises, suggest the directions in which the international monetary system is moving. It will be the purpose of this chapter to review the major problems arising out of the operation of the present system and to suggest how these problems might be resolved in light of recent and foreseeable developments.

The Volume and Composition of Reserves

The proposed SDR facility will give the world a reserve asset which can be managed so as to assure a steady growth in the total volume of international liquidity and trade. It provides an alternative to gold which has been making little or no contribution to world reserves on the one hand, and an alternative to official holdings of reserve currencies without necessarily reducing the volume of world reserves on the other. Thus, if governments choose to shift a portion of their reserve currency holdings into SDRs, the volume of SDRs can be expanded accordingly. In order to insure a steady rise in total reserve assets and to avoid shifts in the composition of reserve asset holdings from suddenly reducing the total volume of liquidity, the new method of reserve creation should combine agreed annual increases in SDRs with special supplements to offset the effects of shifts arising from reductions in reserve currency holdings.[1] Such an arrangement would also cushion (but not fully offset) the effects of a reduction in reserve currency holdings on the reserve assets of the reserve currency countries. So long as the United States continues its policy of converting official dollars into gold, the same rule should apply; any decrease in foreign official dollar holdings should be offset by an increase in SDRs. The United States has approximately 25 percent of the quotas of the IMF, so that if foreign official holdings of dollars decline by $1 billion and this amount were offset by an equivalent increase in SDR allocations, the United States would receive approximately $250 million in additional SDRs.

The implementation of a program for assuring a steady rise in overall reserves will depend mainly upon the willingness of the EEC members, who together possess a veto over the allocation of SDRs, to consent to the management of the SDR facility in accordance with the principles outlined above. While much depends upon the behavior of the U.S. economy and balance of payments, the stake of these countries in an orderly international payments system is so great as to suggest that they will cooperate in such a program. The willingness of other EEC members to vote against France at the Stockholm meeting of the Group of Ten (March 1968) by supporting the proposed amendment to the IMF Articles, which would establish the SDR facility, is most promising. By January 1, 1969, the proposed amendment had been accepted by 27 countries (including the United States) representing 47 percent of the voting power in the IMF.

The Future of Gold

Even those American economists who have been most insistent upon the maintenance of the gold convertibility of the dollar as an essential element in the international monetary system now admit

---

[1] This point was stressed in the Congressional Committee Report, *Guidelines for Improving the International Monetary System—Round 2*, Report of the Subcommittee on International Exchange and Payments, U.S. Congress, Joint Economic Committee (Washington, D.C.: USGPO, December 19, 1967), pp. 6–7.

that SDRs may gradually replace gold as a reserve asset. For example, Robert V. Roosa, who has been a staunch believer in continued gold convertibility of the dollar, recently made the following statement in response to a proposal by Senator Jacob Javits for major changes in U.S. gold policy:

> Nonetheless, it is because I share Senator Javits' feelings that the system must eventually be changed, and that the unique dependence upon the gold-dollar relationship is inappropriate for world finance on the present scale, that I believe every effort should be made to speed up the completion of the process that precedes introduction of the SDRs themselves.[2]

The March 17, 1968, communiqué of the members (now former members) of the London gold pool sets forth in broad terms the likely future role of gold in the international monetary scheme.[3] In this statement, the members agreed that they would not supply gold to the private markets, acquire gold from the private markets, or sell gold to monetary authorities to replace gold sold in the private markets. This agreement suggests that the stock of monetary gold will be frozen at its present level (about $40 billion) and permitted to circulate within an airtight system among monetary authorities. All newly produced gold would flow into the private market; and the market price would fluctuate in response to the demand for industrial uses and private hoarding, and the supply from new gold production and dishoarding.[4] Thus, the price of gold might for a time fall well below $35 per ounce; but in the

---

[2] "A Reaction to Senator Javits' Proposals on Gold Policy," *Banking*, April 1968, p. 108.

[3] See Appendix B for the text of the communiqué.

[4] In the spring and summer of 1968 a controversy arose as to whether the South African government would be required to sell all newly mined gold which it acquired from South African gold mines in the private gold markets, or whether it could sell a portion of this gold either to foreign central banks or to the IMF. Some of the former members of the London gold pool reportedly favored permitting South Africa to sell gold to foreign central banks whenever the price of gold declined to $36 or $37 an ounce, in spite of the fact that such sales appeared to be contrary to the March 17, 1968, decision of the London gold pool members not to purchase gold in the private markets or from new production. The United States government, on the other hand, has

light of the growing industrial demand and slow rate of increase in production, the price of gold might eventually rise well above $35 per ounce. Meanwhile, however, the new SDR system would become permanently established.

As the volume of SDRs expands, gold would constitute a declining proportion of total reserve assets. Moreover, the regulations with respect to the holding of SDRs would prevent countries from reducing their SDR holdings in favor of gold. Also, the proposed IMF amendment provides that a participant may use its special drawing rights to purchase balances of its currency held by another participant, with the agreement of the latter. Thus, the United States might offer to convert dollars presented to it by monetary authorities in either gold or SDRs, at the option of the United States. Under the system outlined above, SDRs would become the virtual equivalent of monetary gold, and while the world would remain officially on the gold standard, the role of the "barbarous relic" would gradually diminish to one of nominal or symbolic significance.

The Problem of Adjustment

An adequate volume of world liquidity and the adoption of a monetary system that would avoid the harmful consequences of sudden shifts by reserve asset holders from one type of reserve asset

---

maintained that all South African gold acquired from new production should be sold in the private markets. In fact, the United States apparently hopes that the free market price of gold might at times fall below $35 an ounce. A related problem is whether the IMF is obliged under the Articles of Agreement to purchase newly mined gold from the South African government at $35 per ounce. Since the Articles of Agreement are not wholly clear on this question, the IMF had not, at the time of writing, made a final decision. Many central bankers evidently believe that if the price of gold were to fall below $35 an ounce, it would tend to impair confidence in the value of their gold reserves. (See "Fowler Urges South Africa to Sell Gold in the Free Market Without Seeking Accords," *The Wall Street Journal*, July 16, 1968, p. 3; "Accord on Sales of Gold Expected," *The New York Times*, July 17, 1968, p. 55; "South Africa Has Already Sold Gold to Central Banks and Free Market," *The Wall Street Journal*, July 19, 1968, p. 3; and "Support of Gold at $35 Indicated," *The New York Times*, August 9, 1968, p. 47.)

into another (e.g., from reserve currencies into gold) would facilitate balance of payments adjustment, but could neither assure adjustment nor provide a substitute for adjustment. To the extent that countries in deficit acquire newly created reserves, they can finance their deficits; but a volume of newly created reserves sufficient to cover any conceivable amount of deficits would be wholly unacceptable to surplus countries. On the other hand, reserves ought to grow at a rate which would enable countries in deficit to get into balance without requiring surplus countries to incur deficits. Thus, deficit countries should be able to achieve equilibrium partly through the expansion of world reserves, and only partly at the expense of the balance of payments of the surplus countries. As was discussed in Chapter 3, an important characteristic of an international monetary system designed to maximize world trade would be to permit balance of payments adjustments by deficit countries without inducing the surplus countries to take measures which would contract their imports or impose restrictions on capital movements.

For most countries, adjustment involves the standard remedies of controlling domestic demand in relation to domestic output, with or without a change in exchange rates, depending upon the causes of disequilibrium. There will also continue to be cases of temporary and reversible disequilibrium, and in these circumstances countries should rely on their reserves (including SDRs) plus borrowing from the IMF and from other sources. However, a special problem exists for the reserve currency countries whose deficits may arise from their intermediation functions as world bankers. In the following paragraphs we shall deal with the balance of payments problems of the two reserve currency countries, the United States and Britain.

The Future of U.S. Balance of Payments

The U.S. balance of payments deficits under the liquidity concept may be traced to a combination of several factors operating in recent years. While all items in the balance of payments are interdependent and individual items cannot be associated with a certain portion of the overall deficit, however defined, we may distinguish three categories of transactions in analyzing the factors contributing to the U.S. deficit. First are the large overseas military expenditures which totaled $4.3 billion in 1967. Second, the U.S. merchandise trade surplus also declined from $6.7 billion in 1964 to $3.7 billion in 1967, and fell to about $1 billion in 1968. Much of this deterioration might well be attributed to the rise in domestic spending relative to domestic output and to some deterioration in the U.S. competitive position in world markets both as an exporter and importer. The third factor is the heavy outflow of private capital in the form of U.S. direct investments and loans abroad. (Much of the government capital outflow has been tied to U.S. exports so that its adverse effect on the U.S. balance of payments, while considerable, has undoubtedly been substantially less than the net outflow of government capital.) A portion of the private capital outflow might be regarded as private intermediation in the sense that it was matched by increases in foreign private holdings of liquid dollar assets and long-term securities in the United States. In the absence of any of these three categories, the U.S. deficit in 1967 ($3.6 billion) would have been modest or nonexistent. While the above analysis is a gross oversimplification of the factors contributing to the U.S. deficit, it does provide some clues as to the nature of the U.S. adjustment problem.

Let us assume that in the future foreign monetary authorities will not increase their holdings of U.S. liquid dollar assets, but will demand gold or SDRs for any additional dollars they may acquire. Under these circumstances, the United States could avoid a loss of reserves only if the entire excess of dollars paid out over dollars received from the export of goods and services were held by private foreign entities in the form of either liquid dollar assets or other dollar investments. Given increased confidence in the dollar (which would be greatly strengthened by the elimination of the gold drain) and a stable and prosperous U.S. economy, annual increases in private holdings of both liquid and nonliquid dollar assets are likely to be substantial. For example, between April 1967 and April 1968 private foreign entities increased their holdings of liquid dollar assets by over $3 billion, and in addition foreigners purchased about $2 billion (net) in U.S. corporate securities, plus substantial amounts of other long-term assets.[5] It is entirely possible that the United States could run an annual deficit of $2 to $3 billion (liquidity concept) without a loss of official reserves or, in other words, without a deficit under the official settlements concept. In addition, large long-term investments in the United States by foreigners would offset an equivalent amount of U.S. private and government capital outflow. These counter-capital flows constitute the essence of the world banker function of the United States. But other adjustments in the U.S. balance of payments would permit this country to export more capital and to do away with the present capital export controls. A reduction in inflationary forces in this country would undoubtedly lead to an improvement in the merchandise account, especially a decrease in imports. Meanwhile, private capital exports will yield a continuously rising stream of dividend and interest payments, which in 1967 totaled well over $6 billion. Finally, our military expenditures abroad could be reduced by a more equitable sharing of the overseas defense burden with our European allies[6] and by a termination of the Vietnam war.

Should the U.S. balance on current account continue to narrow, a change in the exchange value of the dollar might eventually be required. However, as has been noted, it is very difficult for the leading key currency country to devalue. Since most of the rest of the world would not accept an appreciation of their own currency vis-à-vis the dollar, the best approach would be to try to induce a few persistent surplus countries, perhaps the EEC countries as a group, to appreciate their currencies vis-à-vis both the dollar and sterling. However, such a course is presently unwarranted and

[5] In 1966, private foreign entities increased their holdings of liquid dollar assets by nearly $3 billion, and foreigners purchased over $700 million (net) of U.S. corporate securities. The breakdown of foreign holdings of nonliquid dollars between foreign private and official holders is not available to the author. See *Federal Reserve Bulletin*, July 1968, pp. A–74 and A–8.

[6] A recent study by Joseph Aschheim for the Joint Economic Committee of the Congress suggests that Western Europe should compensate the United States for the U.S. defense presence in Germany in the amount of $2 billion. See "The Dollar Deficit and German Offsetting," *The 1968 Economic Report of the President*, Part 4, U.S. Congress, Joint Economic Committee (Washington, D.C.: USGPO, 1968), p. 934.

should be unnecessary if the United States is able to achieve and maintain relative price stability together with a high level of economic performance.

The Problem of Sterling

Britain's role as a world banker has undergone a relative decline since World War II, but sterling remains as an important vehicle currency, and the London capital market, though subject to substantial restrictions on capital exports, plays a significant role as a source of capital for the sterling area and for a number of other countries with close trade and financial ties to Britain. Britain's external sterling liabilities totaled $12.8 billion (equivalent) as of March 1968; in addition, Britain had external liabilities in foreign currencies totaling $11.9 billion.[7] About two-thirds of Britain's external sterling liabilities represent the holdings of foreign monetary authorities, and the remainder constitute holdings of short- and long-term sterling assets by banks and other private entities.[8] While small compared with the $33 billion in foreign liquid liabilities of the United States, Britain's sterling liabilities are large for a country with a GNP less than one-seventh that of the United States. Unlike the United States, whose foreign liquid liabilities have risen by fourfold since 1951, Britain's external sterling liabilities have increased in terms of dollars by only 13 percent since 1951.

Britain's large sterling liabilities have constituted a heavy burden and have contributed to several financial crises during the post-World War II period. While Britain's current account has been in modest surplus during most years since 1951, the surpluses have not been adequate to cover both the private and government capital outflow. Like the United States, Britain has had large overseas military and economic aid commitments, some of which are cur-

---

[7] Against these external liabilities Britain has external sterling claims of $3.4 billion and external claims in foreign currencies of $12.1 billion (as of March 1968), of which $6.0 billion dollars represent dollar assets in the United States. Thus, Britain's external liabilities exceeded its external assets by over $9 billion. Britain's official gold holdings were only $1.5 billion. Data on British external assets and liabilities are found in *International Financial Statistics*.

[8] $4.1 billion of Britain's $8.6 billion in sterling liabilities to foreign central banks represented liabilities to sterling area members (as of March 1968).

rently being withdrawn. When internal or external events affecting Britain's trade balance have occurred, such as dock strikes, the Suez crisis of 1956, or the Middle East war in the summer of 1967, there have been speculative runs on sterling requiring Britain to borrow large amounts from the IMF and from other industrial countries. A series of difficulties in 1967 impairing Britain's trade balance led to a crisis of confidence resulting in the 14.3 percent devaluation of sterling in November of that year. The sterling devaluation, with its attendant loss of over a billion dollars to foreign sterling holders, resulted in a weakening of confidence in the dollar as well and gave rise to the massive flight from currencies into gold during the period from November 1967 to March 1968.

The future role of sterling as a reserve currency will depend upon Britain's making certain adjustments which, in some respects, are similar to those required to strengthen the world banker functions of the United States.[9] First, Britain needs to improve its trade balance. The 1967 sterling devaluation, unlike the sterling devaluation of 1949, was not accompanied by widespread devaluation by other industrial countries and has thus provided Britain with an opportunity to improve its lagging competitive position in world markets. Britain's trade position would also benefit from membership in the EEC. Second, Britain must cut back on its large overseas expenditures or obtain compensation for its overseas defense outlays from European allies. Unfortunately, Britain's withdrawal of military bases in the Middle East and Asia will either leave a defense vacuum to be filled by Russia and China or will require a larger commitment by the United States, unless Western Europe, Japan, and other industrial countries assume greater obligations for free world defense. Finally, Britain needs to remove the constant threat to its international solvency presented by large sterling liabilities. Britain's reserves are not only small in relation to its sterling liabilities—its official gold and convertible currency reserves were $2.7 billion as of March 1968—but Britain has borrowed large amounts from the IMF and under swap agreements with other

[9] For an excellent discussion of Britain's future prospects and requirements see Robert V. Roosa, "Where is Britain Heading?" *Foreign Affairs*, April 1968, pp. 503–518.

countries for dealing with recent financial crises. Britain's total external foreign currency liabilities ($11.9 billion as of March 1968) exceed its foreign currency and gold assets.

Many students of British finances have recommended that Britain be assisted in funding or in otherwise liquidating a substantial portion of its short-term sterling liabilities.[10] Indeed, the Anglo-American Financial Agreement of 1946, under which the United States loaned $3.75 billion to Britain to enable it to restore sterling convertibility, included a provision according to which Britain would undertake to fund a substantial portion of its sterling balances.[11] However, Britain was unable to reach agreements for funding these balances with the sterling area countries which at that time held the bulk of the $15.5 billion in sterling balances. As of March 1968, the monetary authorities of the sterling area countries held $4.1 billion in sterling balances, while another $4.1 billion represented liabilities to the monetary authorities of developed countries; most of the remaining $4.6 billion in external sterling liabilities were held by private foreign banks, firms, and individuals. One method of dealing with that portion of the sterling balances held by governments would be to exchange them for SDRs in the Fund and then require Britain to liquidate the sterling balances held by the IMF over a period of, say, 50 years, plus a modest rate of interest. Another approach that has been under discussion would be for Britain to arrange a long-term loan from the Group of Ten.[12] Some of the privately held sterling liabilities are in the form of

[10] Under the original Triffin Plan, sterling balances would be exchanged by foreign holders for IMF deposits. Robert Roosa has recommended assistance for funding of a large portion of Britain's sterling liabilities. See Robert V. Roosa, *Monetary Reform for the World Economy* (New York: Harper and Row, 1965), pp. 100–110.

[11] See *Anglo-American Financial Agreement*, U.S. Department of State, September 1945.

[12] "Sterling Area's End? Britain Seeks Long-Term Loan to Let Allies Pull Out Reserves from London," *The Wall Street Journal*, June 24, 1968, p. 1. In September 1968, a $2 billion stand-by credit was made available to Britain through the BIS and underwritten by the central banks of 12 nations. The purpose of the credit was to enable Britain to give a dollar guarantee on a portion of her sterling liabilities to sterling area countries. The arrangements with the sterling area members are regarded as a movement toward the gradual withdrawal of sterling as a reserve currency.

long-term obligations, while a substantial portion, perhaps £1 to 1½ billion are required as working balances for financing sterling transactions.

Even if sterling were no longer an important reserve asset for members of the sterling area, the pound might continue to serve as a vehicle currency for a significant portion of the world's international transactions.[13]

Britain's institutions for financing trade, the existence of British branch banks throughout the sterling area and in nonsterling countries, the existence of a number of international commodity markets centered in London, and Britain's close economic ties with its former dependencies, all suggest that sterling will play an important role in world trade and financial transactions for decades to come. Moreover, if confidence can be restored in the pound and greater freedom of capital transactions permitted, the London capital market can provide an important intermediation function in which institutions and individuals abroad can hold relatively liquid funds in London, funds which can, in turn, be used for long-term capital investments in other areas of the world.

The Less Developed Countries and International Monetary Reform

The less developed countries have an enormous stake in the creation of a world monetary order that will minimize restrictions on world trade and capital movements. Balance of payments difficulties of the developed countries have resulted in restrictions on imports of the products of the less developed countries and in limitations on both foreign aid and private capital exports to developing countries. The recent cuts in U.S. foreign aid appropriations are due in no small measure to U.S. balance of payments difficulties, and U.S. government capital export controls have been imposed on direct investments in the developing countries as well as in the developed countries.[14] Balance of payments difficulties of aid

[13] As has already been noted in Chapter 1, the use of sterling as a vehicle currency has declined significantly in recent years.

[14] In January 1968, the U.S. government limited new net capital transfers to the developing nations to 110 percent of the 1965–1966 average of direct

donors have also been partly responsible for the increase in the practice of tying aid to the exports of the donor countries. Aid-tying has been applied to both bilateral aid and to aid made available through international institutions.[15]

The reserves of most developing countries are also inadequate for dealing with the fluctuations in their export receipts arising particularly from sharp movements in world market prices of primary commodities. The SDR allocations to the developing countries will assist them in dealing with these fluctuations without an impairment of their development programs.[16] However, these additions to the reserves of the developing countries will make only a modest contribution to their requirements and will need to be supplemented by special compensatory financing such as that recommended by the World Bank's recent report to UNCTAD.[17] The willingness of the United States and other developed countries to establish a compensatory financing facility for dealing with unexpected shortfalls in export earnings of developing countries will depend in considerable measure upon the achievement of an adequate international monetary reform.

A number of proposals have been made for the creation of reserve assets to be used in the first instance to finance foreign aid transfers to the developing countries. For example, a Congressional committee has recently proposed that a portion of the SDRs created by the Fund be used to purchase long-term bonds of the International Development Association for use in making loans to

---

investment. In addition, limitations were imposed on the reinvestment of foreign earnings. See U.S. Treasury Department, *Maintaining the Strength of the United States Dollar in a Strong Free World Economy* (Washington, D.C.: USGPO, January 1968), pp. 97–98.

[15] For a discussion of costs of aid-tying, see Raymond F. Mikesell, *The Economics of Foreign Aid* (Chicago: Aldine, 1968), pp. 246–254.

[16] Triffin objects to the proposed distribution of SDRs on the basis of existing IMF quotas. He suggests that it is economically and morally indefensible that three-fourths of the SDRs are to be allocated to the developed (rich) countries while only about one-fourth would be allocated to the 82 less developed members of the IMF. Robert Triffin, *Our International Monetary System: Yesterday, Today and Tomorrow* (New York: Random House, 1968), p. 194.

[17] See International Bank for Reconstruction and Development, *Supplementary Financial Measures* (A Study Requested by the United Nations Conference on Trade and Development), December 1965.

developing countries.[18] Professor Triffin, whose own plan provided for the channeling of XIMF deposit credits through an international agency, has also recommended that SDRs be employed for the support of international undertakings such as development financing.[19] On the other hand, the linking of foreign aid to reserve asset creation might impair cooperation among developing countries in implementing the new SDR facility. The function of an international monetary system which generates an adequate volume of liquidity is not to induce directly an increase in international transactions. Its function is, rather, to establish an environment for the maximum expansion of trade and capital movements consistent with the optimum allocation of resources. Under an ideal international monetary system with each country operating in accordance with proper economic and financial policies, no country should be required to impose artificial restrictions on its imports or impair its economic growth by deflationary action in order to maintain reasonable external balance. The leading developed countries, including the key currency countries, should maintain free private international capital markets. In addition, under such a system developed countries should be able to provide whatever foreign assistance they decide they can afford in terms of giving up real resources, without tying their assistance to their exports and without fear of impairing their balance of payments. Of course, these conditions could not be achieved by international monetary reform alone; they would require a high degree of internal and external price flexibility and ideal monetary and fiscal management, including appropriate exchange rate policies on the part of all developed countries. But a proper reform of the international monetary system could help move the world in this direction.

[18] *Guidelines for Proving the International Monetary System—Round 2*, pp. 7–9.

[19] Triffin, *Our International Monetary System: Yesterday, Today and Tomorrow*, p. 195.

Addendum on the U. S. Balance of Payments in 1968

On the basis of preliminary data reported by the U.S. Department of Commerce in February 1969,[20] the United States had a small surplus in its balance of payments on the liquidity basis of about $190 million in 1968 as contrasted with a deficit of $3,570 million in 1967. On the official reserve transactions basis, the United States had a surplus of $1,660 million as contrasted with a deficit of $3,400 million in 1967. This improvement was due entirely to movements in the capital accounts, notably a sharp rise in foreign purchases of U.S. private securities. The U.S. surplus on merchandise account declined to less than $100 million as compared with a surplus of nearly $3.5 billion in 1967. This decline reflected a $6.3 billion increase in imports and a $2.9 billion rise in exports. Although the increase in foreign investments in the United States indicated continued confidence in the dollar, many elements in the complex of capital movements which gave rise to the improvement in the overall balance of payments are regarded as nonrecurrent. Consequently, the Nixon Administration decided to retain for the time being the controls over the outflow of U.S. capital.

[20] "The U.S. Balance of Payments for Fourth Quarter and Year 1968," *Press Release*, U.S. Department of Commerce, February 1969.

Appendix A

Proposed Amendment
of Articles of Agreement
of the International Monetary Fund
by the Executive Directors of the Fund,
April 1968

THE SPECIFIC LANGUAGE *of the proposed amendment to the Articles of Agreement of the IMF[1] proposed by the Executive Director of the IMF in April 1968 for implementing the resolution, passed by the Board of Governors at its annual meeting in Rio de Janeiro in September 1967, is highly technical and legalistic. Rather than reproduce this document (which is available on request from the IMF), it would appear to be more useful to most of the readers of this book to reproduce an analysis and interpretation of the proposed amendment prepared by the U.S. Treasury Department and presented by Secretary of the Treasury Henry H. Fowler to the Committee on Banking and Currency, U.S. House of Representatives, on May 1, 1968. Secretary Fowler's statement on the proposed amendment follows.*

[1] See International Monetary Fund, *Proposed Amendment of Articles of Agreement, A Report by the Executive Directors to the Board of Governors,* Washington, D.C., April 1968.

Main Features of Special Drawing Rights Facilities

Nature of the Amendment

The Executive Directors of the Fund have proposed a single, integrated Amendment to the Articles of Agreement of the IMF and this Amendment must be accepted or rejected by countries in its entirety; the approach of accepting or ratifying some parts of the Amendment, while rejecting others, is not open. The integrated Amendment does, however, contain material of two different types:

1. A series of provisions that will introduce modifications into a number of features of the *existing* Articles of Agreement, so as to make changes in the regular or traditional operations of the Fund that are being proposed as a result of the experience of the Fund or in order to be sure the regular Fund operations and the new special drawing rights facility fit together into a consistent whole; and
2. A new set of additional Articles, Articles XXI through XXXII together with four new Schedules, which will be added on to the existing twenty Articles and five Schedules and will furnish the legal framework for implementing the new special drawing rights facility within the institutional set-up of the International Monetary Fund.

Let me describe how the new arrangements will work, starting with the procedure to make the Amendment legally effective, proceeding to a discussion of the special drawing rights system, and finally touching on the most important of the proposed changes in the regular Fund.

Procedure for Making the Amendment Effective

The new provisions are to become effective by the procedure of amending the Fund's Articles of Agreement. The Proposed Amendment must first be approved by the Fund's Board of Governors, consisting of one Governor from each of the 107 Fund members.

Approval requires a majority of the weighted votes cast, and the votes cast must represent the equivalent of a quorum of the total voting power of the Fund Governors, this being established as two-thirds of the total voting power. The Executive Directors have determined that this vote will be completed May 31. Approval by the Governors does not constitute, as a matter of law, acceptance or ratification of the Amendment on behalf of any member government. I have cast an affirmative vote as the U.S. Governor of the Fund, after consultation with the National Advisory Council on International Monetary and Financial Policies.

After approval by the Board of Governors, the governments of members of the Fund will be asked formally whether they accept the Amendment. It is at this stage that formal governmental acceptance is involved, and prior legislative authorization by the Congress is required. The Amendment in its entirety will become legally effective, pursuant to the provisions of the Articles of Agreement governing amendments, when 60 percent of the members having 80 percent of the total voting power have accepted it by formally notifying the Fund to that effect.

When this has occurred, the Amendment will be fully effective as a body of law. A further requirement is provided for, however, before the members of the Fund will be in a position to decide to activate the special drawing rights facility to create and allocate new reserve assets. This is to form a body of *participants* in the new Special Drawing Account, through which the SDR system will be administered within the Fund. Each member of the Fund has the right to become a participant in the Special Drawing Account, but no member is legally obligated to do so, even if the member has ratified the Amendment. In order to become a participant in the Special Drawings Account, a Fund member must deposit with the Fund a document setting forth that it has taken all steps necessary to enable it to carry out all of its obligations as a participant. Only when members having 75 percent of the Fund quotas have thus become participants can decisions of the participants in the new scheme be taken. This procedure for substantial participation protects countries from incurring financial obligations against their will, and also guards against the theoretical possibility that a very few countries would quickly become participants and would make decisions under the new scheme that would be opposed by the great majority of countries that had not yet completed the procedure to become participants. At the same time, the 75 percent participant requirement, while relatively high, would still enable the scheme to move ahead even if substantial delays were to be encountered on the part of some countries in completing the steps to become participants. In practice, of course, it is expected that nearly all countries will want to handle acceptance of the Amendment by becoming a participant simultaneously and in a single procedure, and that is what the United States proposes to do.

Initial Activation to Create SDR

I hope that the SDR facility will be in place and in a position to take decisions at an early date—hopefully by the end of 1968, but certainly in any event by early in 1969. It will then be feasible to initiate the procedure looking toward the first activation of the SDR system. Here a word on the question of timing and quantities is in order. Neither the timing of the first activation, nor its amount, can be foreseen clearly at this time. Both of these aspects are, under the Amendment, to be matters for consultation and decision when the system has come into force and the Amendment contains very carefully drafted provisions governing these procedures. Decisions to activate the system will normally provide for annual creation and allocation of a specified amount of SDR to participants over a five-year period ahead, but these standard features of a decision can be altered. So far as any *ceiling* or outer limit on the initial capacity of the SDR mechanism to create and allocate SDR, it is understood that members of the Fund wishing to become participants will seek financial authority of *not less than* what is necessary for them to meet their obligations when SDR allocations to them have reached 50 percent of their quotas when they become participants. If that were to be generally adopted as the initial upper limit, the SDR mechanism would have the capacity to create and allocate as much as $10.5 billion of SDR before participants would have to seek additional legislative authority. But there is also a widespread feeling that countries will wish to treat SDR in their domestic financial legislation in the same way they treat official holdings of gold and foreign exchange, and to the extent this practice is followed, there would be no ceiling on the financial authority of participants in the new facility to create and allocate such amount of SDR as would command the necessary weighted majority vote.

In the process of reaching a decision on the timing and amount of creation and allocation of SDR, the Managing Director of the Fund will play a central role. He must conduct such consultations as will enable him to ascertain that there is broad support among participants for moving ahead, and must satisfy himself that his proposal will be consistent with specified principles governing creation and allocations. For all such decisions, these principles are that there is a long-term global need to supplement existing reserve assets, that doing so will promote the general purposes of the Fund, and that the quantity proposed will avoid both economic stagnation and deflation as well as excess demand and inflation in the world. In addition, for the first decision to allocate, three special considerations must be taken into account:

1. A collective judgment (referring to the required 85 percent vote) that there is a global need to supplement reserves;
2. The attainment of a better balance of payments equilibrium; and
3. The likelihood of a better working of the adjustment process in the future.

All of the principles and considerations laid out to govern decisions on creation and allocation are matters for careful judgment and consultation in the light of developments as seen when decisions are in the process of being shaped, and none of them can be reduced to precise statistical formulations.

Any decision to allocate SDR must be made on the basis of a proposal by the Managing Director. To become effective, the proposal must be concurred in by a majority of the weighted votes of the Fund's Executive Directors and then adopted by 85 percent of the weighted voting power in the Board of Governors. In decisions relating exclusively to the Special Drawing Account, only the votes of participants in that Account are taken into account. It may be said here that, although no decision to create and allocate special drawing rights can be made except on the basis of a proposal of the Managing Director, the Board of Governors will have authority to amend any proposal before adopting it by 85 percent of the total voting power of participants. Moreover, if the Managing Director has failed to put forward a proposal—whether to start the first activation or later—either the Board of Governors or the Executive Directors may, by a simple majority of the weighted voting power of the participants, make a formal request for him to present one. The Managing Director must then comply within six months, unless he ascertains in the process of his consultations that there is no proposal which he can make that would be consistent with the principles and considerations governing allocation and also has broad support among participants; in this event, he must submit a report on the situation to both the Board of Governors and the Executive Directors. So, you see, there are a number of checks and balances built into the procedure for reaching very carefully considered and widely supported decisions as to the timing and amount of creation of SDR.

All SDR to be created will be allocated to participants in the scheme, and only to them. The allocation to participants will be on the basis of their quotas in the Fund on the date of each decision to allocate. Since the relative size of quotas in the Fund is, at least in principle, determined as an approximation to the relative international economic and financial size of Fund members, this basis for allocation appeared fair and reasonable. In fact, decisions to create and allocate will be expressed in terms of a common percentage of Fund quotas for each participant. Since Fund quotas are presently about $21 billion, the creation of $1 billion of SDR would be expressed as 4.76 percent of quotas assuming all Fund members were participants in the SDR facility. Out of each $1 billion of SDR created, the allocation to the United States would be about $246 million, and that to the six members of the Common Market about $179 million.

Opting Out

Considerable public discussion has taken place on the question of "opting out," and I should explain here what the Amendment means in this respect. As I have said, every member of the Fund has the right to become a participant, but no member is obligated to do so. Thus, any country that wishes may stay out of the SDR facility entirely. The question of "opting out," however, refers to the choices that are open to a country, once it has become a participant and is thus a voting member of the group of countries able to adopt decisions to create and allocate SDR. The facts on opting out are these:

1. If the Fund Governor of a participant has voted in favor of a decision to allocate SDR at a specified annual rate over a period of five years ahead, and that decision has been adopted by the required 85 percent majority, the participant is obligated to receive all the allocation of SDR provided for in the decision and to undertake any and all the obligations associated with these allocations—the participant cannot "opt out";

2. If the Fund Governor of a participant has *not* voted in favor of (that is, has abstained or voted against) a decision to allocate SDR, and the decision has nonetheless been adopted by the required 85 percent majority, the participant then has a choice. It may elect to receive the allocations decided upon, notwithstanding the failure of its Governor to vote in favor of the decision. Or, it may elect not to receive the allocations decided upon. If it wishes not to receive the allocations, and to avoid the corresponding acceptance obligations which I shall discuss presently, it must notify the Fund of this decision prior to the first annual allocation of SDR under the decision. This action to refuse to receive allocations decided upon by the required 85 percent majority is what is meant by "opting out." Since only participants whose Governors have not voted in favor of the decision to allocate have the right to

opt out, and the decision must be supported by 85 percent of the total voting power of participants in order to be adopted, the amount of reduction in SDR creation that would result from any exercise of the right to opt out could not exceed, at a maximum, about 15 percent of the amount contemplated by the original proposal.

3. A country that has opted out may be permitted by the Fund to "opt back in" and thus to resume receiving allocations under the same decision from which it previously opted out. In case of such a change of heart, the participant must request the Fund to permit it to opt back in and the Fund may do so by a majority of the votes in the Executive Board. It is understood that the attitude of the Fund toward a request to "opt back in" will be a sympathetic one, though of course such sympathy could be reversed if a participant showed an irresponsible approach toward the matter. Once a participant had "opted back in," it would not have the right to opt out again under the same allocation decisions; opting out again would only be possible at the time of a subsequent five-year decision to allocate SDR. In addition, opting back in applies only to receiving those annual allocations that occur after opting back in has occurred; it is not possible to receive retroactively the annual allocations already foregone.

Use and Transfer of SDR

Once received through the allocation process, SDR can be used by participants in a manner broadly the same as the use of traditional reserve assets—gold and foreign exchange—when these are used to make settlements arising from balance of payments developments or to support one's currency in the exchange markets. There are, however, rules governing use of the SDR in transfers among monetary authorities. While quite complex in their detail, these rules have a few main purposes:

1. To avoid instability in the system by avoiding the use of SDR solely to change the composition of reserve holdings;

2. To channel transfers of SDR in such manner as to treat all participants on the basis of the same standards, to encourage wide and active entering into operations of the SDR scheme among participants, and to encourage familiarity with, and confidence in, the SDR as an instrument for making settlements;

3. To permit careful use of the SDR in transactions between participants and the regular or traditional Fund, just as traditional reserves are used; and

4. To encourage participants, by a modest obligation, not to simply pay out all their SDR and then forsake further activity in the SDR mechanism.

SDR are not to be used by presenting them to the Fund itself for conversion, since under the SDR mechanism (unlike the mechanism of the regular Fund) the Fund will not hold a currency pool related to SDR. Rather, SDR are to be used among participants by transferring them directly from one participant to the other through appropriate debits and credits entered on the books of the Special Drawing Account. Thus, SDR will in fact have many of the characteristics of legal tender for use in transfers among the monetary authorities of participants. Transfers among participants will generally be in return for convertible currency, and the participant transferring SDR will have full guarantees of receiving a convertible currency conveniently usable in its circumstances in return for the SDR transferred.

To illustrate concretely how SDR will normally be used, let me borrow a practical and concrete example recently used by Mr. Schweitzer, the Managing Director of the Fund.

Let us assume that the Board of Governors has by an 85 percent majority taken the decision to activate the scheme and that for the first basic period, as we call it, an amount of special drawing rights equivalent to $1 billion a year is to be allocated. That is just an example. Now let us suppose that a hypothetical country, let us call it country A, has a quota in the Fund representing one percent of total quotas; this at present would be a quota of some $200 million. When the allocation is made, the Fund would credit this country in the

Special Drawing Account with an amount of special drawing rights equal to $10 million, for if the country had one percent of participants' total quotas, it would receive one percent of the allocation. Country A could at that time add these drawing rights to its reserves because it would be entitled to use them, without any conditions, in case of need.

Let us now assume that country A has a need and wants to use, let us say, half of its drawing rights to meet this need. In order to do so, it would have to convert them into a usable currency. It would, therefore, approach the Fund and ask to what participating country it should transfer the rights in order to get an equivalent amount of convertible currency. The Fund would at all times maintain a list of participating countries whose balance of payments and reserve situations were considered satisfactory; and from this list it would designate one or more appropriate countries to provide currency against special drawing rights. Let us assume that in this instance Germany and Italy are chosen for equal amounts. The Fund would accordingly notify Germany and Italy that it was crediting them, in the Special Drawing Account, with the equivalent of $2½ million each in special drawing rights and that they should credit the central bank of country A in their respective books with $2½ million of deutsche marks and $2½ million of lire. At the same time the Fund would debit Country A an amount of drawing rights equivalent to $5 million.

As a result of these transactions, $5 million of special drawing rights in the assets of country A would have been replaced by $5 million of convertible currencies which country A could then use freely for any purpose; and Germany and Italy would have increased their assets in the form of drawing rights by $2½ million each. Country A would be charged a moderate rate of interest—foreseen as 1½ percent, at least initially—on its use of drawing rights; and Germany and Italy would be paid interest at the same rate. I should remind you also that the special drawing rights would have an absolute gold value guarantee. Country A, as long as it used on average over a period of five years no more than 70 percent of the special drawing rights allocated to it by the Fund, would have no reconstitution obligation.

I have talked about the rights of country A in using the special drawing rights. I should mention also that the obligation of Germany and Italy or any other participant to accept drawing rights over and above their allocation and to provide currency in return would extend only up to a point where they had accepted drawing rights equal in value to twice the amount allocated to them by the Fund, unless of course they agreed to hold more.

Use of the SDR by the United States

Let me now mention how the SDR allocated to the United States are expected to be used by us. Basically, there are three possibilities:

1. Our preference is, if our balance of payments and reserve position permits, to hold on to SDR allocated to us, so as to build up our reserve holdings in this form over a secular period of time. U.S. reserves have suffered a severe decline over a period of many years, and are now no more than average among all Fund members when measured against the size of our imports or our total international transactions—and such comparisons do not make allowance for the special feature of our short-term liabilities in the form of dollar balances held by other monetary authorities and by private foreign holders. We would welcome growth in our reserves stemming from allocation of SDR, and if this were further supplemented by the channeling of SDR transfers from other participants to us under the SDR provisions, that would also be very welcome.

2. If the United States satisfied the test of "need-to-use" SDR, due to developments in its balance of payments or in its over-all reserves, the United States could use SDR to purchase official dollar balances from another participant, provided that other participant agreed to this use. This method of use would enable the United States to use SDR, in appropriate cases, in a manner very much analogous to the way in which we—as the principal market intervention currency in the international monetary system—use our traditional reserves of gold. I should stress two points, however. This method of use involves a *voluntary transaction* and thus is dependent upon the other

party to the transaction being willing to agree to it. And, being provided for as a voluntary transaction on both sides, such a transaction would not involve the Fund playing the role of "SDR traffic director" to determine to which other participant the transfer should be made.

3. It would also be open to us, if we preferred it or if other countries did not agree to voluntary transactions of the kind just described, to use SDR for transfers under the general provisions. In this event, the "need-to-use" requirement would have to be met, just as before, but the transfer of SDR from the United States would be to one or more other participants designated by the Fund under its standard criteria, rather than to a participant chosen by the United States. The United States would receive convertible currency from the participant designated by the Fund; most likely it would be dollars, but if not it would be convertible into dollars, and the net result would be that the United States would have used SDR to purchase dollars from countries selected by the Fund, rather than from countries selected by the United States itself.

Other Features of SDR Use

In concluding these descriptive comments on use of SDR in transfers, I have made reference to the role of the Fund as "traffic director" in channeling flows of SDR in such a manner as to make the system operate smoothly and well. Four other factors should be covered under the heading of use of SDR to make transfers among monetary authorities:

1. The central obligation of participants is to provide convertible currency in exchange for SDR transfers to them from other participants. This central obligation is the main feature that assures the practical value of SDR as a reserve asset. The obligation is sufficiently important that any breach of it is made subject to the most severe penalties elaborated in the SDR provisions. Hence, a country holding SDR for use in a future period of need will have all possible assurances that it can effectively and smoothly

make use of SDR when the need presents itself. The obligation to accept SDR and pay convertible currency in return is not unlimited; it does not extend beyond the point at which a participant's holdings of SDR are three times the amount allocated to it. Thus, this basic obligation means that a participant is committed to accept, against convertible currency, an amount of SDR equal to twice the allocation to it. The size of this obligation to accept SDR when they are presented is, in our view, adequately large to give a practical assurance that SDR held by any participant can effectively be transferred to other participants under the terms of the Amendment. At the same time, the limitation on the acceptance obligation gives assurance to a country in surplus that it will not wind up holding all of the SDR in existence. Thus, on both sides, the acceptance obligation offers equitable and practical assurances.

2. In the rules governing transfer, the provision of a convertible currency against SDR, at a determined exchange rate, is fully and carefully provided for. There are no ambiguities or loop-holes in the system for determining to which other participant a transfer of SDR should be made, what convertible currency is to be provided in return, how to convert that currency into the currency desired by the country making the transfer, and what precise exchange rate is to be applied to each of these transactions. It is a fully determinate system, and each participant wishing to use SDR at any given time will have a clear and precise answer to any question as to how to go about it and what amount he will receive in the currency he wishes. Again, the assurances to the prospective user of SDR are complete.

3. It was thought desirable to provide some modest safeguards against the possibility that a participant would simply pay out the SDR received in allocation, and then abstain from further transactions. This would hardly constitute effective and proper participation in a system designed to provide for the ebb and flow of reserves as

payments positions shifted. Accordingly, a provision was included in the Amendment providing for obligations to "reconstitute" holdings of SDR, once they had been used. The basic requirement—which is applicable only for the period of the first activation and can be changed or abrogated later by an 85 percent majority—is that averaged over a time period of the most recent five years, average holdings of SDR should not fall below 30 percent of the amount allocated to the participant. This obligation would, of course, not become operative at all if a participant did not use more than 70 percent of his allocations. Nonetheless, all of a participant's allocations may be used from time to time without difficulty or conditions, so long as the *average* holdings over five years do not fall below 30 percent of allocations. This is not an onerous obligation. Detailed provisions are included in the Amendment by which the Fund will assist participants to acquire SDR needed to meet this obligation, and, if necessary, a participant will have the obligation and entitlement to obtain any SDR needed to fulfill the obligation in a transaction with the General Account (that is, the regular Fund) or, if all else fails, from another participant specified by the Fund.

4. Provisions also exist under which SDR can be used in a number of transactions between participants and the General Account of the Fund, through which the Fund will henceforth conduct its traditional functions. The most important of these transactions will enable participants to repay previous drawings from the Fund partly or wholly with SDR. The Fund will also be able to supply SDR, instead of a national currency, to a country making a drawing from the General Account, if the drawing member agrees.

Holders Other Than Participants

Finally, I should mention a provision enabling the Fund to impart some flexibility to the SDR system. As previously mentioned, only participants in the Special Drawing Account will be able to receive allocations of SDR. The regular Fund will be able to receive transfers of SDR from participants under certain defined circumstances, to hold them and to make use of them in defined ways. In addition, the Fund will have authority to prescribe other countries, which are not participants, and certain types of international bodies as authorized holders of SDR, by a decision requiring an 85 percent majority of the voting power of participants. The prescription so made must include terms and conditions consistent with the other provisions governing SDR. Under this power, the Fund could empower a non-Fund member such as Switzerland to enter into SDR transactions. It could also authorize the BIS or a regional monetary agency in Latin America to enter into such transactions. However, only institutions performing one or more functions of a central bank for more than one member of the Fund could be authorized in this way; other international institutions, such as those engaged in development financing, could not be authorized as holders of SDR or to engage in SDR transactions.

Modifications in the Traditional Fund

Under the Amendment proposed by the IMF Executive Directors, the familiar traditional operations of the Fund will be carried on in the new "General Account," while SDR business will be carried out through the "Special Drawing Account." The Amendment also contains proposals to modify certain of the provisions of the existing Articles of Agreement. These changes fall under six heads, constituting those proposals for change which have been agreed upon, out of a rather longer and more difficult group of proposals that at one time had achieved some status among the EEC countries.

A. Change in Voting Procedure for Quota Increases

At present, any change in quotas in the Fund requires an 80 percent majority of the voting power in the Board of Governors. Under the new proposal, this required majority will be raised to 85 percent for those quota increases resulting from a general review of the adequacy of quotas. In addition, any decision to depart from the standard requirement that 25 percent of quota increases be paid in gold, or to mitigate the effects of this gold payment, will also require an 85 percent majority in the Board of Governors. Such decisions related to payment for quota increases, to the extent the Articles of Agreement permitted them, could previously be taken by the Executive Directors by a simple majority of the voting power. It was asserted that this change was "logically linked" to the 85 percent voting requirement for creation of SDR, since quota increases in the traditional Fund could, to a limited extent, create additions to international liquidity.

B. Uniform Change of Par Values

A second change, which some countries also saw as "logically linked" to the 85 percent voting majority in the SDR system, concerns a hypothetical Fund decision to make a uniform proportionate change in par values of currencies—or in other words, to change the price of gold. Since additional reserves could also be created by such a decision, it was argued this decision should also be made subject to an 85 percent majority. Presently, such a decision can be made by the Fund Governors by a simple majority of the voting power, provided that every country with 10 percent or more of the Fund quotas concurs; this means that the United Kingdom and the United States are the only countries able to veto such a decision. Since the new proposal, requiring an 85 percent majority, makes a decision to change the price of gold more difficult to achieve, the United States was able to go along with this proposal. In addition, if a uniform proportionate change in par values were decided upon, the Fund has the authority to decide *not* to maintain the gold value of its assets. Previously such a decision could be made by a simple majority by the Executive Directors; under the Proposed Amendments, such a decision will be possible only by an 85 percent majority in the Board of Governors.

C. Interpretation of the Articles of Agreement

The Fund has authority to make final and binding interpretations of its own Articles of Agreement. Such interpretations can initially be made by the Executive Directors by a majority of the weighted votes; an interpertation so made can then be appealed to the Board of Governors whose decision, by a majority of the voting power, is final. Although the right of interpretation has been used with care and responsibility, and only one appeal has been made to the Board of Governors, it was argued by some that the existing procedure for interpretation, decided solely by a weighted voting system, could create dangers that should be avoided by a more traditional form of judicial review. The provision contained in the Proposed Amendment will still utilize the Executive Directors as the initial tribunal for interpretation and will retain interpretation within a procedure internal to the Fund. A Committee of Governors will be established to which an appeal can be lodged from an interpretation by the Executive Directors. The size of the Governors' Committee on Interpretation, its composition, and the majority by which it will decide appeals has not yet been decided and will be determined subsequently by an appropriate provision of the Fund By-Laws. It has been decided, however, that voting within the Governors' Committee will be on the basis of one vote per member of the Committee, as is usual in judicial procedures. It is to be expected that it will be decided the Governors' Committee can reverse an interpretation by the Executive Directors only by a qualified majority vote—I would think by a rather high proportion of the votes in the Committee. The decision of the Committee, in turn, will be able to be appealed to the full Board of Governors, and overturned then by an 85 percent majority of the total voting power. Governors of the Fund who are members of the Committee will be able to appoint alternates, and it is assumed those who will actually conduct any judicial review as members of the Committee will be highly qualified legal officers of member governments. The new procedure for interpretation will apply only to new questions of interpretation.

D. Automaticity of Drawing Rights in the "Gold Tranche"

The gold tranche drawing rights of Fund members—that is, drawing rights arising from their gold subscriptions plus their "net creditor" positions corresponding to the net amount of their currency subscription drawn from the Fund by other members—will be made legally unchallengeable under the Proposed Amendment. This, in effect, represents a legal codification of a de facto policy and practice that the Fund has followed since February 1952. Several consequential changes in provisions are included to carry out this purpose. In addition, the Fund will in future have the right to eliminate the existing one-time transaction charge, which is required to be paid for all drawings from the Fund, on drawings in the gold tranche. Further, "net creditor" positions in the regular Fund (or "super gold tranche" positions as they are sometimes called) are in future to earn a remuneration (essentially an interest return) which is initially set at 1½ percent per year; the rate can be varied within the range of 1 to 2 percent by a majority of the voting power, and to a point beyond these limits, if conditions require it, by a majority of 75 percent. All of these changes relating to the status of the gold tranche in the Fund are designed to improve its position as a reserve holding, in a manner comparable to that being accorded to the SDR.

E. Conditions on Credit Tranche Drawings

Drawings from the regular Fund in the credit tranches—that is, drawings beyond amounts arising from a member's gold subscription or a previously accumulated "net creditor" position—have always been subjected to policy conditions by the Fund. This has been justified on the ground that the Fund's resources are intended to "revolve" and to finance temporary swings in balance of payments positions, so that the policy conditions applied by the Fund should be designed to encourage countries to cope with and reverse the payments problems that have led to their drawings on the Fund. This approach to credit tranche drawings is now to be codified in the Articles of Agreement by provisions which clearly indicate that credit tranche drawings from the regular Fund are to be made for temporary payments difficulties and that the policies of countries making credit tranche drawings must be examined to determine whether they are such as to render their use of credit tranche drawings temporary and reversible. It is important to note, however, that under these modifications, the Fund will retain full authority to adapt its policies on credit tranche drawings and that it is not necessary to make the existing policies and practices more stringent in order for them to conform to the terms of the Proposed Amendment.

F. Automatic Repurchases

Repurchases are transactions by which Fund drawings are reversed or "repaid." In recent years, more than 90 percent of such repayments have been through repurchases at scheduled maturities within 3–5 years from the corresponding drawings, or by virtue of other members making drawings of the currency of the country needing to repay. In addition, however, the Articles provide for mandatory repurchases in circumstances where the reserves of the country with drawings outstanding have been rising, and it was thought desirable to modify these highly technical provisions to bring them more up to date. In the Articles as they now stand, a net reserve concept (that is, gross holdings of reserve assets minus short-term liabilities in the country's own currency to foreign official holders plus foreign banks) was used in determining reserve increases or decreases for this purpose; in the Proposed Amendment, a gross reserve concept is to be used for this purpose, in the same way that gross reserves are normally used as the basis of most economic analysis in modern thinking. Several new features are to be placed in the formula for determining mandatory repurchases, as follows:

1. The basic formula is to take account of repurchases effected by other means during the Fund's financial year, to reduce repurchases calculated under the mandatory formula. This has not been the case under the existing provisions.
2. Mandatory repurchases are to be subject to the following limits:
   a. They will not be due in an amount that will reduce the repurchasing member's gross reserve holdings below 150 percent of its Fund quota. The comparable limit in the existing Articles is that a repurchasing member's net reserves will not be reduced below 100 percent of its Fund quota.

    b. Any calculated amount in excess of 25 percent of the repurchasing member's Fund quota in a given year will be postponed until the end of the following Fund financial year. There is no analogous limitation in the existing provision.

3. The Fund will have discretion to disregard, in its calculation of reserve increases and the resulting mandatory repurchase obligations, reserve holdings arising out of swap transactions.

Finally, the existing provisions on mandatory repurchase can result in repurchases being calculated in a currency which the Fund cannot accept because the country issuing that currency itself has drawings outstanding from the Fund; in that event (which is the situation for mandatory repurchases calculated in either U.S. dollars or sterling at present) the calculated repurchase is abated (or in other words, completely set aside). It appeared undesirable to continue this practice, and in the future, under the Proposed Amendment, such calculated repurchases will have to be carried out in other currencies acceptable to the Fund.

Appendix B

Meeting of Governors of Central Banks Contributing to Gold Pool: Communiqué

THE GOVERNORS of the Central Banks of Belgium, Germany, Italy, the Netherlands, Switzerland, the United Kingdom, and the United States met in Washington on March 16 and 17, 1968, to examine operations of the gold pool, to which they are active contributors. The Managing Director of the International Monetary Fund and the General Manager of the Bank of International Settlements also attended the meeting.

The Governors noted that it is the determined policy of the U.S. Government to defend the value of the dollar through appropriate fiscal and monetary measures and that substantial improvement of the U.S. balance of payments is a high-priority objective.

They also noted that legislation approved by Congress makes the whole of the gold stock of the nation available for defending the value of the dollar.

They noted that the U.S. Government will continue to buy and sell gold at the existing price of $35 an ounce in transactions with monetary authorities. The Governors support this policy and believe it contributes to the maintenance of exchange stability.

The Governors noted the determination of the U.K. authorities to do all that is necessary to eliminate the deficit in the U.K. balance of payments as soon as possible and to move to a position of large and sustained surplus.

Finally, they noted that the governments of most European countries intend to pursue monetary and fiscal policies that en-

SOURCE: *Federal Reserve Bulletin*, March 1968, p. 254.

147

courage domestic expansion consistent with economic stability, avoid as far as possible increases in interest rates or a tightening of money markets, and thus contribute to conditions that will help all countries move toward payments equilibrium.

The Governors agreed to cooperate fully to maintain the existing parities as well as orderly conditions in their exchange markets in accordance with their obligations under the Articles of Agreement of the IMF. The Governors believe that henceforth officially held gold should be used only to effect transfers among monetary authorities and, therefore, they decided no longer to supply gold to the London gold market or any other gold market. Moreover, as the existing stock of monetary gold is sufficient in view of the prospective establishment of the facility for Special Drawing Rights, they no longer feel it necessary to buy gold from the market. Finally, they agreed that henceforth they will not sell gold to monetary authorities to replace gold sold in private markets.

The Governors agreed to cooperate even more closely than in the past to minimize flows of funds contributing to instability in the exchange markets, and to offset as necessary any such flows that may arise.

In view of the importance of the pound sterling in the international monetary system, the Governors have agreed to provide further facilities which will bring the total of credits immediately available to the U.K. authorities (including the IMF standby) to $4 billion.

The Governors invite the cooperation of other central banks in the policies set forth above.

Appendix C

World Gold Demand and Supply

IN RECENT YEARS, the private demand for gold has been rising faster than gold production in South Africa and other gold-producing countries outside the U.S.S.R. Russian gold sales have added to new supply but such sales have behaved erratically, and there were no Russian sales during 1967. (See Figure C–1.) Free world gold production declined from an estimated $1,445 million in 1966 to $1,410 million in 1967, or by about 2 percent. Since 1964, private gold absorption has exceeded annual gold production, and in 1966 and 1967 gold absorption exceeded both new gold production and Soviet sales, so that official gold holdings declined. (See Figure C–2.)

Of the estimated $2.5 billion of gold going into private holdings and industrial uses in 1967, an estimated $0.6 billion was consumed in the United States and other industrial countries for industrial uses, such as the electronic and aerospace industries and the fabrication of gold articles. Industrial uses have been increasing rapidly (close to 20 percent per annum in the United States, and about 10 percent per annum in eleven other industrial countries). In the United States industrial uses reached an estimated $250 million in 1967 as against only half that amount in 1962. Thus, in the absence of a substantial rise in the price of gold, industrial demand alone is likely to absorb all new gold production within a few years.

Demand for gold for private hoarding has risen very rapidly in response to expectations of a rise of the official price of gold. If the public becomes convinced that an increase in the official price of

FIGURE C-1
Estimated Supplies of Gold

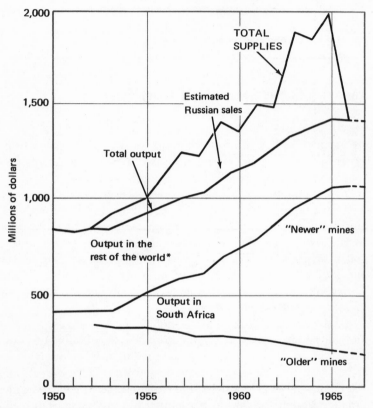

*Excluding the U.S.S.R., other Eastern European countries, mainland China, and so on.
SOURCE: First National City Bank of New York, *Monthly Economic Letter*, January 1968

gold is not likely to take place in the near future, much of this demand may subside. But there is, nevertheless, a constant demand for gold for hoarding purposes which is likely to continue regardless of the outlook for change in the official price. Hence, even if a restoration of confidence in the dollar and sterling and other major currencies takes place and this is accompanied by some liquidation of speculative gold holdings, it is likely that the long-run

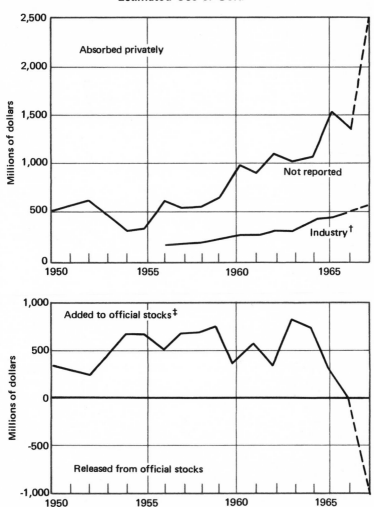

FIGURE C-2
*Estimated Use of Gold**

*Excluding the U.S.S.R., other Eastern European countries, mainland China, and so on.
†Reported by the United States and other industrial countries.
‡Excludes, for 1965, $150 million and, for 1966, $75 million reportedly purchased by mainland China; this amount is likewise excluded in the upper part of the chart.
SOURCE: First National City Bank of New York, *Monthly News Letter*, January 1968.

private market price of gold will be upward. This will be true even if the major industrial countries hold to their agreement of March 1968 not to acquire any more gold for official holdings from the private market including new gold production.[1]

[1] See "Annual Gold Review," *Monthly Economic Letter* (First National City Bank of New York), January 1968, pp. 8–11; see also Herbert B. Woolley, "New Patterns, New Outlook, for World Gold," *Engineering and Mining Journal*, October 1967 (reprinted, New York: McGraw-Hill, 1967).

Bibliography

BOOKS AND ARTICLES

Allen, William R., and Clark Lee Allen (eds.). *Foreign Trade and Finance: Essays in International Economic Equilibrium and Adjustment* (New York: Macmillan, 1959).

Altman, Oscar L. "Eurodollars: Some Further Comments," IMF *Staff Papers*, March 1965.

———. "Foreign Markets for Dollars, Sterling, and Other Currencies," IMF *Staff Papers*, December 1961.

———. "International Liquidity and the Balance of Payments," IMF *Staff Papers*, November 1965.

———. "Professor Triffin, International Liquidity and the International Monetary Fund," in Seymour E. Harris (ed.), *The Dollar in Crisis* (New York: Harcourt, Brace & World, 1961).

———. "Recent Developments in Foreign Markets for Dollars and Other Currencies," IMF *Staff Papers*, March 1963.

Angell, James W. "The Organization of the International Monetary System: An Alternative Proposal," *Economic Journal*, December 1961.

Aschheim, Joseph. "The Dollar Deficit and German Offsetting," *The 1968 Economic Report of the President*, Part 4, U.S. Congress, Joint Economic Committee (Washington, D.C.: USGPO, 1968).

Aubrey, Henry G. *The Dollar in World Affairs* (New York: Praeger, 1964).

Balogh, T. "International Reserves and Liquidity," *Economic Journal*, June 1960, pp. 357–377.

Bernstein, Edward M. "The Bernstein Approach," in Randall Hinshaw (ed.), *Monetary Reform and the Price of Gold: Alternative Approaches* (Baltimore: Johns Hopkins Press, 1967).

———. "Further Evolution of the International Monetary System," *Moorgate and Wall Street*, Summer 1965, pp. 51–70.

Birnbaum, E. A. *Changing the U.S. Commitment to Gold* (Princeton, N.J.: International Finance Section, Princeton University, November 1967).

Bloomfield, Arthur I. *Monetary Policy Under the International Gold Standard: 1880–1914* (New York: Federal Reserve Bank of New York, October 1959).

Canterbery, E. Ray. "A Skeptical View of the 'Band' Proposal: A Comment," *The National Banking Review*, Vol. IV, June 1967.

Cassell, Francis. *Gold or Credit? Economics and Politics of International Money* (New York: Praeger, 1965).

Condliffe, J. B. *The Commerce of Nations* (New York: W. W. Norton, 1950).

Coombs, Charles A. "Conversations on International Finance," *Monthly Review* (Federal Reserve Bank of New York, August 1963).

———. "Treasury and Federal Reserve Foreign Exchange Operations," *Monthly Review* (New York: Federal Reserve Bank of New York, March 1968).

Despres, Emile, Charles P. Kindleberger, and Walter S. Salant. "The Dollar and World Liquidity: A Minority View," *The (London) Economist*, February 5, 1966.

DeVries, Margaret. "Multiple Exchange Rates: Expectations and Experiences," IMF *Staff Papers*, July 1965.

Feis, Herbert. *Europe: The World's Banker 1870–1914* (New Haven: Yale University Press, 1930).

Fleming, J. Marcus. "International Liquidity: Ends and Means," IMF *Staff Papers*, December 1961.

———. "The Fund and International Liquidity," IMF *Staff Papers*, July 1964.

———. "Effects of Various Types of Fund Reserve Creation on Fund Liquidity," IMF *Staff Papers*, July 1965.

Friedman, Milton. "The Case for Flexible Exchange Rates," *Essays in Positive Economics* (Chicago: University of Chicago Press, 1953).

Gilbert, Milton. *Problems of the International Monetary System* (Princeton, N.J.: International Finance Section, Princeton University, 1966).

Goldstein, Henry N. "A Further Comment on an Aspect of the 'Band' Proposal," *The National Banking Review*, Vol. IV, June 1967.

———. "Further Thoughts on Official Support of the Forward Exchange Rate," *Quarterly Journal of Economics*, August 1966.

Grubel, Herbert G. "The Benefits and Costs of Being the World Banker," *The National Banking Review*, Vol. I, December 1964.

Grubel, Herbert G. (ed.). *World Monetary Reform, Plans and Issues* (Stanford: Stanford University Press, 1966).

Haberler, Gottfried. *Money in the International Economy: A Study in Balance-of-Payments Adjustment, International Liquidity, and Exchange Rates* (Cambridge, Mass.: Harvard University Press, 1965).

Halm, George N. *The "Band" Proposal: The Limits of Permissable Exchange Rate Variations* (Princeton, N.J.: International Finance Section, Princeton University, January 1965).

Hansen, Alvin Harvey. *The Dollar and the International Monetary System* (New York: McGraw-Hill, 1965).

Harris, Seymour E. (ed.). *The Dollar in Crisis* (New York: Harcourt, Brace & World, 1961).

Harrod, Sir Roy. *Reforming the World's Money* (London: Macmillan, 1965).

Hawkins, Robert G. (ed.). *Compendium of Plans for International Monetary Reform* (New York: Graduate School of Business Administration, New York University, 1965).

Heilperin, M. S. "The Case for Going Back to Gold," *Fortune*, September 1962.

Hinshaw, Randall (ed.). *Monetary Reform and the Price of Gold* (Baltimore, Md.: Johns Hopkins Press, 1967).

Holmes, Allan R., and Francis H. Schott. *The New York Stock Exchange Market* (New York: Federal Reserve Bank of New York, 1965).

Johnson, Harry G. "Major Issues in Monetary and Fiscal Policies," *Federal Reserve Bulletin*, November 1964.

———. "Towards a General Theory of the Balance of Payments," *Readings in International Economics*, Vol. XI (Homewood, Ill.: Richard D. Irwin, 1968).

———. *The World Economy at the Cross Roads: A Survey of Current Problems of Money, Trade, and Economic Development* (Oxford: Clarendon Press, 1965).

Kenen, Peter B. *Reserve-Asset Preferences of Central Banks and Stability of the Gold Exchange Standard* (Princeton, N.J.: International Finance Section, Princeton University, 1964).

Kindleberger, Charles P. *Balance-of-Payments Deficits and the International Market for Liquidity* (Princeton, N.J.: International Finance Section, Princeton University, 1965).

Kriz, Miroslav A. *Gold: Barbarous Relic or Useful Instrument?* (Princeton, N.J.: International Finance Section, Princeton University, October 1967).

———. *Gold in World Monetary Affairs Today* (Princeton, N.J.: International Finance Section, Princeton University, 1959).

Lary, Hal B., and Associates. *The United States in the World Economy* (Washington, D.C.: U.S. Department of Commerce, 1943).

Lerner, Abba P. "Let's Get Rid of Our Cross of Gold," *Challenge*, April 1964.

Lutz, Friedrich August. *The Problem of International Liquidity and the Multiple-Currency Standard* (Princeton, N.J.: International Finance Section, Princeton, 1963).

Machlup, Fritz. "The Cloakroom Rule of International Reserves: Reserve Creation and Resources Transfer," *Quarterly Journal of Economics*, August 1965.

———. "Credit Facilities or Reserve Allotments?" Banca Nazionale de Lavoro *Quarterly Review*, Rome, June 1967. (Reprinted in Princeton International Finance Section Reprint Series.)

———. *International Monetary Economics: Collected Essays* (London: Allen & Unwin, 1966).

———. "The Need for Monetary Reserves," Banca Nazionale de Lavoro *Quarterly Review*, Rome, September 1966.

———. *Plans for Reform of the International Monetary System*, rev. ed. (Princeton, N.J.: International Finance Section, Princeton University, 1964).

———. "Relative Prices and Aggregate Spending in the Analysis of Devaluation," *American Economic Review*, June 1955.

Mayer, Lawrence A. "The World's Freest Money Market," *Fortune*, April 1968.

Meade, J. E. *The Balance of Payments* (London: Oxford University Press, 1955).

———. "The International Monetary Mechanism," *The Three Banks Review*, September 1964.

Mikesell, Raymond F. *The Economics of Foreign Aid* (Chicago: Aldine, 1968).

———. *Foreign Exchange in the Postwar World* (New York: Twentieth Century Fund, 1954).

———. *Inflation in Latin America*, Subcommittee on American Republics Affairs, Committee on Foreign Relations, U.S. Senate (Washington, D.C.: USGPO, September 1967).

———. "United States as World Banker," *The National Banking Review*, December 1966.

Mundell, Robert A. *The International Monetary System: Conflict and Reform* (Montreal: Canadian Trade Committee, Private Planning Association of Canada, 1965).

———. "A Theory of Optimum Currency Areas," *American Economic Review*, September 1961.

Nurkse, Ragnar. *International Currency Experience* (Geneva: League of Nations, 1944).

Rueff, Jacques. "The Rueff Approach," in Randall Hinshaw (ed.), *Monetary Reserves* (Washington, D.C.: American Enterprise Institute for Public Policy Research, 1966).

Pizer, Samuel and Frederick Cutler. "U.S. Exports to Foreign Affiliates of U.S. Firms," *Survey of Current Business*, December 1965.

Reisman, Guenter and Edwin F. Wigglesworth. *The Challenge of International Finance* (New York: McGraw-Hill, 1966).

Romanis, A. "Balance of Payments Adjustment Among Developed Countries," IMF *Staff Papers*, March 1965.

Roosa, Robert V. *Monetary Reform for the World Economy* (New York: Harper and Row, 1965).

———. "Where is Britain Heading?" *Foreign Affairs*, April 1968.

Roosa, Robert V. and Fred Hirsch. *Reserves, Reserve Currencies, and Vehicle Currencies: An Argument* (Princeton, N.J.: International Finance Section, Princeton University, 1966).

Rueff, Jacques. "The Rueff Approach," in Randall Hinshaw (ed.), *Monetary Reform and the Price of Gold: Alternative Approaches* (Baltimore: Johns Hopkins Press, 1967).

Rueff, Jacques and Fred Hirsch. *The Role and the Rule of Gold: An Argument* (Princeton, N.J.: International Finance Section, Princeton University, 1965).

Salant, Walter S., and Associates. *The United States Balance of Payments in 1968* (Washington, D.C.: The Brookings Institution, 1963).

Scitovsky, Tibor. *Requirements of an International Reserve System* (Princeton, N.J.: International Finance Section, Princeton University, 1965).

Snider, D. A. *Optimum Adjustment Process and Currency Areas* (Princeton, N.J.: International Finance Section, Princeton University, October 1967).

Sohmen, Egon. *Fluctuating Exchange Rates: Theory and Controversy* (Chicago: University of Chicago Press, 1961).

———. *International Monetary Problems and the Foreign Exchanges* (Princeton, N.J.: International Finance Section, Princeton University, 1963).

Stamp, Maxwell. "The Stamp Plan—1966 Version," *Moorgate and Wall Street*, Autumn 1962.

Stein, J. L. *The Nature and Efficiency of the Foreign Exchange Market* (Princeton, N.J.: International Finance Section, Princeton University, October 1962).

Swoboda, Alexander K. *The Eurodollar Market: An Interpretation,* Essays in International Finance, No. 64 (Princeton, N.J.: International Finance Section, Princeton University, February 1968).

Tew, Brian. *The International Monetary Fund: Its Present Role and Future Prospects* (Princeton, N.J.: International Finance Section, Princeton University, 1961).

Triffin, Robert. *The Balance of Payments and the Foreign Investment Position of the United States* (Princeton, N.J.: International Finance Section, Princeton University, 1966).

————. *The Evolution of the International Monetary System: Historical Reappraisal and Future Perspectives* (Princeton, N.J.: International Finance Section, Princeton University, 1964).

————. "The Coexistence of Three Types of Reserve Assets," Banca Nazionale del Lavoro *Quarterly Review,* Rome, June 1967.

————. *Contingency Planning for U.S. International Monetary Policy,* Subcommittee on International Exchange and Payments, Joint Economic Committee, U.S. Congress (Washington, D.C., December 1966).

————. *Gold and the Dollar Crisis,* rev. ed. (New Haven: Yale University Press, 1961).

————. "The International Monetary System," *Moorgate and Wall Street,* Summer 1965.

————. *Our International Monetary System: Yesterday, Today and Tomorrow* (New York: Random House, 1968).

————. *The World Money Maze: National Currencies in International Payments* (New Haven: Yale University Press, 1966).

Wasserman, Max J., *et al. International Finance* (New York: Simmons-Boardman, 1963).

Williamson, John H. *The Crawling Peg* (Princeton, N.J.: International Finance Section, Princeton University, December 1965).

Willis, George A., and Fred L. Springborn. *The Need for International Reserves* (Washington, D.C.: U.S. Treasury Department, September 1967).

Yeager, Leland B. *International Monetary Relations* (New York: Harper and Row, 1966).

————. "A Skeptical View of the 'Band' Proposal," *The National Banking Review,* Vol. IV, March 1967.

DOCUMENTS

The Balance of Payments Statistics of the United States: A Review and Appraisal, Report of the Review Committee for Balance of Payment Statistics to the Bureau of the Budget (Washington, D.C.: USGPO, 1965).

Group of Ten, Study Group on the Creation of Reserve Assets, *Report to the Deputies of the Group of Ten* (Washington, D.C.: USGPO, 1965).

International Bank for Reconstruction and Development, *Supplementary Financial Measures,* December 1965.

International Monetary Arrangements: The Problem of Choice (Princeton, N.J.: International Finance Section, Princeton University, 1964).

International Monetary Fund, *Annual Report 1965* (Washington, D.C., 1965).

————, *Annual Report 1966* (Washington, D.C., 1966).

————, *Annual Report 1967* (Washington, D.C., 1967).

————, *Articles of Agreement of the International Monetary Fund* (Washington, D.C., 1946).

————, "Communiqué of the Ministerial Meeting of the Group of Ten," *International Financial News Survey*, April 5, 1968.

————, *Proposed Amendment of the Articles of Agreement*, A Report by the Executive Directors to the Board of Governors (Washington, D.C., April 1968).

"Ministerial Statement of the Group of Ten and Annex," *Federal Reserve Bulletin*, August 1964.

U.S. Congress, Joint Economic Committee, *Guidelines for Improving the International Monetary System: Report* (Washington, D.C.: USGPO, 1965).

U.S. Congress, Joint Economic Committee, *Guidelines for Improving the International Monetary System—Round 2*, Report of the Subcommittee on International Exchange and Payments of the Joint Economic Committee (Washington, D.C.: USGPO, December 19, 1967).

U.S. Congress, Joint Economic Committee, *Guidelines for International Monetary Reform*, Hearings, July 27–29, 1965, 89th Cong., 1st sess. (Washington, D.C.: USGPO, 1965).

U.S. Congress, Joint Economic Committee, "Statement Submitted by Professor Emile Despres," *New Approach to United States International Economic Policy*, Hearings before the Subcommittee on International Exchange and Payments of the Joint Economic Committee, 89th Cong., 2nd sess. (Washington, D.C.: USGPO, September 9, 1966).

U.S. Congress, Joint Economic Committee, *The United States Balance of Payments: Perspectives and Policies*, 88th Cong., 1st sess. (Washington, D.C.: USGPO, 1963).

U.S. Congress, Joint Economic Committee, *The United States Balance of Payments: Statements by Economists, Bankers and Others on the Brookings Institution "The United States Balance of Payments in 1968,"* 88th Cong., 1st sess. (Washington, D.C.: USGPO, 1963).

U.S. Department of State, *Anglo-American Financial Agreement*, September 1945.

U.S. Library of Congress, *Gold and the United States Balance of Payments Deficit* (Washington, D.C.: USGPO, 1961).

U.S. Treasury Department, *Maintaining the Strength of the United States Dollar in a Strong Free World Economy* (Washington, D.C.: U.S. Treasury Department, 1968).

Index